D1102597

HOW TO PHOTOGRAPH
PEOPLE

by RACHEL BRAVERMAN & JON TARRANT

FOUNTAIN BOOKS

HOW TO PHOTOGRAPH PEOPLE

First Edition 1991

by Rachel Braverman and Jon Tarrant

Designed by Jo Tapper
Typeset by GCS
Printed in Hong Kong by Regent Publishing Services

ISBN 0 86343 350 2

Published by
FOUNTAIN PRESS
Queensborough House
2 Claremont Road
Surbiton
Surrey KT6 4QU

The mention of particular manufacturers and their products and the use of pictures of
such products in this publication is solely for illustration and example. This publication is
not sponsored in any way by such manufacturers, nor have the contents of this book
been reviewed or seen by any of the manufacturers whose products are mentioned
herein. Information, data and procedures in this book are correct to the best of the
authors' and the publisher's knowledge. Because use of this information is beyond the
authors' and the publisher's control, all liability is expressly disclaimed. Specifications,
model numbers, operating procedures, etc. may be changed by a manufacturer at any
time and may therefore not always agree with the contents of this book.

*Photographing people can mean anything from the candid
frontispiece to the home studio father and daughter portrait shown
on the cover. This book takes a wide-ranging look at the ways in
which people can be photographed, and breaks away from the
old-fashioned idea that portraiture means moody black and white
headshots. Frontispiece by Jon Tarrant, cover photograph by
Rachel Braverman.*

CONTENTS

Portraiture gives the photographer unlimited opportunities to use his or her imagination. Taking this picture took about 10 minutes, but the preparation and later manipulation were done over a period of weeks.

INTRODUCTION

People are the world's most popular subjects for photographs. Everybody can be a good subject for a picture, young or old, wherever they come from, and almost whatever they are doing.

In this book, we aim to give you a better understanding of the techniques you can use to photograph people. Even the most basic snapshot can be greatly improved by taking a little care. But it is not just a book of absolute rules. Portrait photography is about far more than a tight head and shoulders shot taken in a studio.

The first three chapters look at general techniques as they can be applied to portraiture. These are followed by chapters which cover particular aspects of photographing people, from character studies in the studio to candids and action. The final chapters are designed to help you develop your own style for photography and show your pictures to their best advantage.

We hope that after reading this book, your pictures will be more imaginative, more creative and technically better.

Jon Tarrant and Rachel Braverman

1: EQUIPMENT AND FILMS

INTRODUCTION

Modern photography tends to be equipment oriented. Every gadget that comes on the market seems to promise the solution to yet another photographic problem. But these problems have always had their solutions. The difference is that now it is all so much easier. When equipment gives the photographer more time to concentrate on the creative aspects of picture taking, it is worth the investment. The aim of this chapter is to help you choose the equipment which will be of most use to you and to suggest some thoughts about equipment in general.

WHAT TYPE OF CAMERA?

As far as serious amateur photography is concerned, there are three types of camera worth considering; the sophisticated compact, the 35mm SLR, and medium format.

Compact cameras
Compact cameras are excellent for snatching candid shots. They are easy to use, but what you gain in speed, you lose in flexibility.

There are three aspects to consider when choosing a compact camera; focusing, exposure and flash. If you want to take more than snapshots with a compact camera, it must have the ability to be focused. It is very difficult to be creative with a fixed-focus camera. Autofocus cameras usually assume your subject is in the middle of the frame, which limits your scope for composition. A very useful feature, therefore, is the focus lock, which means that you can focus on your subject, then recompose the picture without changing the focusing. Some compact cameras also offer autofocus override. This means that you can set your compact camera to focus at infinity, which is useful if you are taking pictures through glass, where you might otherwise end up with a sharp picture of the pane itself rather than the scene beyond.

The degree of sophistication of auto-exposure tends to match that of the focusing. Fixed-focus cameras usually have fixed exposure – another reason to avoid them. We would recommend cameras with an exposure lock, which works in the same way as the focus lock.

Many cameras have a built-in flash. Again, it is useful to be able to override this, for example, when taking silhouettes.

Other features to look out for are built-in zoom lenses, automatic DX-coded filmspeed

Carrying a compact camera made it easy to capture this picture of a boy asleep on a bus.

setting and automatic film advance, all of which can come in handy. Since all compact cameras rely on batteries, you should make sure that the camera you choose uses batteries that are readily available, and always carry spares.

Medium format
'Medium Format' is a general description of cameras using 120 roll film. This produces negatives or slides of 6 × 4.5 cm, 6 × 6 cm or 6 × 7 cm. Which of these sizes you choose depends on which shape you prefer. There is not a great deal of difference in image quality.

As the size of the negative increases, so does the weight and expense of the equipment. Medium format cameras are much more unwieldy than 35mm. They are physically slower; you sometimes have to press two levers to wind on the film and recock the shutter. Because of their weight, they are almost always used with a tripod, so they can be cumbersome on location. However, their very bulk gives the photographer authority, which can be useful on formal occasions.

Another major disadvantage is high cost. It is sometimes possible to hire medium format equipment or you may be able

to borrow gear from a camera club.

Medium format comes into its own in the studio because it offers a lot of control. The ability to change film backs means you can swap rolls of film halfway through without losing frames or putting exposed films at risk. A Polaroid film back is especially useful for checking lighting and posing as you go along. You can also see what you are doing very clearly because the large viewfinder, and bigger negatives, make the results easier to see at each stage. Finally, there is a psychological advantage if you want to sell your work. It is still true that a lot of people think of medium format as the high quality, professional option, although this attitude is changing slowly.

35mm SLR cameras

One of the arguments sometimes cited in favour of medium format cameras is that their larger film size means less enlargement which means film defects are not exaggerated and dust on the negative is not so obvious. While all this is true, the high quality of modern films and processing

35mm was the ideal format for this picture, as it is light enough to be carried around, and flexible enough to cope with more imaginative ideas. Photograph by Brian Fanning

equipment makes the argument rather academic. The authors have had 60″ × 40″ prints made from 35mm negatives, and the quality has been surprisingly good. Accurate exposure, a firm support for the camera, and a high quality lens, can make prints from 35mm films that are every bit as good as many prints taken from larger format negatives. 35mm is much cheaper and more flexible than medium format.

Choosing between different makes is a personal matter. It is very important that the camera feels comfortable for you, and this is something that can only be assessed by your handling different models. There is also the question of technical features that the camera may have, and how important or useful these are. All that is really required is that the camera can support a lens at one end, and film at the other, but in addition most modern cameras have exposure metering built in. A camera that had just these features would represent the most basic type of modern 35mm camera, such as the very robust Nikon FM2.

Amongst the useful extra features that more sophisticated cameras may offer are:

● Advanced metering systems which can identify difficult

lighting situations, and automatically correct for them.

● Through the lens flash metering for accurate exposure with suitably dedicated flashguns.

● Depth of field preview to view what will appear sharp in the final picture, according to the aperture set.

CAMERA SYSTEMS

A camera need not be just a single piece of equipment; it can be part of a larger system of accessories, including lenses, flashguns, and motordrives. For this reason, it is important that any camera you decide to buy can be fitted with all the accessories that you may need in the future. Unfortunately, this is very difficult to judge, because you cannot know for sure what you may want in years to come. One way to safeguard yourself is to buy a camera made by one of the big name manufacturers, who tend to design their cameras as part of a complete system at the outset. This brings other considerations into play, because different manufacturers have different criteria in designing their systems. Olympus, for example, have particularly light and tough cameras, and are also well-known for the high quality of their close-up

accessories. Minolta are very much into high technology, with autofocus and flash systems which tend to lead other manufacturers. And Nikon, much beloved by professional photographers, are the only manufacturer to have kept a constant lens mount design. A lens that was built for the original 1962 Nikon F can still be used on the latest Nikon F4 – a claim that no other manufacturer can match.

SELECTING LENSES

The quality of the lens limits how good your final picture quality can be. It makes sense, therefore, to get the best lenses you can. This need not mean the most expensive ones. 50mm standard lenses, which were once almost automatic accompaniments to new camera bodies, are easy to make, and tend to be of high optical quality. They also have wide maximum apertures (usually f/1.8), making them easy to focus in dim lighting, and also giving them great potential for differential focusing.

The ideal portrait lens
One of the general rules in photography is that there is an ideal lens for doing portrait work. This is based on typical perspectives when viewing the prints, compared to how we

Pictures taken with 28mm, 50mm and 135mm (top to bottom).

13

see people in everyday situations. Portraits are often quite tightly framed head and shoulder poses, and displayed prints are usually enlarged to moderate sizes (between 10″×8″ and 12″×16″), then viewed from a metre or so. The result of these generalisations, is that the ideal portrait lens is defined as one having a focal length twice that of the film diagonal. In the case of 35mm cameras, which have a film diagonal of 43mm, the ideal portrait lens should have a focal length of about 86mm. It is no coincidence that many portrait photographers do in fact use 85mm or 90mm lenses. All the major camera manufacturers have lenses in this category, and there are also several well-acclaimed lenses made by independent manufacturers.

Wide angle lenses

Whereas portrait lenses are most suited to tighter than normal compositions, there are other situations when you will want to create more space within the picture than a standard lens will allow. Lenses which do this are called 'wide-angle', the most common focal lengths being 35mm, 28mm

This picture was taken with a standard 50mm lens and the print trimmed to remove distracting elements.

and 24mm. Of these, the 35mm is really very similar to the standard 50mm lens, except that it gets a bit more in. Pictures taken with 35mm lenses look very natural, and are often indistinguishable from those taken with standard lenses. 28mm lenses, on the other hand, have a definite distorting effect. They can focus closer than standard lenses, and exaggerate the separation between foreground and background when used in this way. They also tend to keep more of the picture sharp because of their greater depth of field at a given aperture. This is even more true for 24mm lenses, but here the distortion tends to become a feature in itself, and there is a danger that it can distract from the subject being photographed.

If it is a matter of choosing just one lens, the 28mm is probably your best option. Alternatively, you could get the 35mm, and then plan to add one of the other lenses soon after.

Telephoto lenses

The generally-accepted definition of a telephoto lens is one which takes in less than the standard lens and which seems to close in on distant objects. We will use that definition here, although telephoto strictly means a lens which is shorter than its focal length. The two major uses for telephoto lenses are to provide a very narrow depth of field, and to close in on a distant subject. The degree to which these effects can be achieved depends on the lens focal length, with those in the range 135mm to 300mm being most useful.

Zoom lenses

When looking at the prices of lenses, and weighing up the bulk that several represent, it is tempting to turn to zoom lenses as an alternative. It is no longer true to say that zooms are of much poorer optical quality than fixed focal length lenses. There are times when zoom lenses really do make sense, and although reducing the weight of your kit could be one reason, expense is not another. A good zoom lens can cost as much as several normal lenses. Cheaper versions often have considerably smaller maximum apertures, making them harder to focus and less useful for differential focusing.

Zoom lenses also have an important psychological disadvantage. If you stumble upon a scene which will make a good background, it is all too easy to compose your picture simply by zooming the lens until you get it all in. Whereas with fixed focal length lenses you need to give some thought

to which lens would be best, and would be more likely to move around in search of the best viewpoint. Another aspect of this same problem is that it is easy to forget what focal length the zoom is set to, and therefore to be unaware of what shutter speed you should be using to avoid blur caused by camera shake.

The effect of maximum aperture

The size of the maximum aperture (indicated by the f number) determines both how easily and how widely a lens can be used. Larger apertures, described by smaller f-numbers, give much brighter images in the viewfinder, and can also provide narrower depth of field if required. Since modern lenses are all focused at maximum (brightest) aperture, which is also associated with the narrowest depth of field, wider aperture lenses promote more critical focusing. If the lens is set to the widest aperture when the picture is taken, you will be able to make maximum use of differential focusing – where the main subject is pin-sharp and both the foreground and background are out of focus. By setting smaller apertures, represented by larger f-numbers, the effect of differential focusing can be reduced, but wide maximum aperture lenses will still benefit

The dreamy effect comes from a combination of grainy film (uprated Tri-X) and a Cokin diffuser.

from a bright viewfinder during focusing. Using lenses with reduced maximum apertures (including many cheaper zoom lenses), means a dimmer viewfinder, and greater restrictions on the use of creative focusing.

FLASHGUNS

A flashgun is, perhaps, the least well understood – and least well used – piece of photographic equipment. Fortunately, it is one area where technology really can make life a lot easier, by taking over the difficult task of assessing correct exposures.

Features to look out for on a good flashgun include:

● Maximum power – This limits the ultimate flexibility of the flashgun. A (metres at ISO 100) guide number of 30 is the minimum for handling a wide variety of situations. Less powerful flashguns can be sufficient for indoor use, but more power is required for some special effects.

● Dedication – to allow camera and flashgun to exchange information automatically. This can range from exposure control, to automatic zooming of the flash head to match the focal length of lens, or zoom setting, being used.

● Cable connector – to allow the flashgun to be used away from the camera hot shoe whilst keeping full dedication.

● Flash head movements – to allow the light to be directed onto walls or ceilings for softer lighting effects.

● Auto exposure – included on all dedicated flashguns, but provided as a separate feature on less sophisticated models. Look for a choice of several aperture options.

● Manual exposure – gives maximum control over lighting and sometimes offers fast recycling mode for use with motor drives.

OTHER ACCESSORIES

Having acquired the bare essentials (camera, lenses and flashgun), you may wonder what other equipment might be useful. The sort of accessories you might consider depends on the sort of photography you prefer. For candids, a right-angle adaptor which enables you to shoot pictures in one direction while pointing the camera in another, could be handy. For sports photography, a longer focal length lens would be sensible, and in the studio some proper lighting

The blue cast caused by exposing tungsten film in daylight has been used to set the mood of the picture. The same picture shot on normal film is very much less striking.

equipment gives you much more flexibility. But in all cases, there are some general accessories that can prove helpful. A selection of these is given on page 20.

FILM

Film should always be bought with a specific purpose in mind. Try to anticipate what sort of things you will be photographing, under what lighting, and to what use the

pictures will be put. Slide film, for example, is very inconvenient for showing family and friends, but is preferred by publishers. Black and white film is the best for recording tones, textures and shapes. It is also simpler to process and print than colour film, so is more suited to the home darkroom.

Colour negative films
The most commonly used films are those giving colour negatives and prints. They are cheap, readily available, easy to use and convenient to show to others. Although there may seem to be many different films, there are a few which stand out as being particularly good. Consumer tests have found that most people pick out prints taken from Konica SR-G 100, as those which look the best. Many professional portrait photographers, however, use Kodak VPS III because it gives pleasing skin

ACCESSORY	BRIEF DESCRIPTION OF USES
Light meters	For measurement of light
Reflection	Measures light reflected from subject
Incident	Measures light falling onto subject
Spot meter	Can measure both light and subject contrast
Filters	To modify image colour/contrast/sharpness
Polarizer	Reduces reflections, and darkens blue sky
Diffusing	Overall softening of image
Softar	Diffuses highlights, giving halo effect
Blue	For natural colours when using daylight film under tungsten lamps (e.g. Wratten 80A)
Orange	For natural colours when using tungsten film in daylight (e.g. Wratten 85A)
Warm-up	Straw coloured, giving tanned skin tones
Reflectors	To modify lighting
White	Subtle lightening of shadows. used close-up
Gold	Lightens shadows and warms skin tones, used at medium distances
Silver	To lighten a small area, very bright, used from far away
Black	To block out unwanted light

tones with good detail in both shadows and highlights.

There has always been debate about which ISO rating gives the best results, and it is true that slower films have smaller grain, but the fact is that modern films are so good that grain is not a reason for making your choice unless you want to do very big enlargements. Fuji Super HG 400, for example, has the smallness of grain more often attributed to ISO 100 films. It is significant that some of the newest films are being marketed not for their smallness of grain, but for their faithful colour rendition. When fine grain really is important, Kodak Ektar films are the ones to use. They do, however, need much more careful exposure than other general purpose films, and are not recommended for casual use.

Care needs to be taken to avoid reflections when photographing people wearing glasses.

Colour slide films

Slide films have a greater density range between highlights and shadows than negative films. They record colour more accurately and offer various options for special effects during processing. The most punchy prints are taken from slides, and printed on Ilford's exceptional Cibachrome papers.

Choosing a slide film is more critical than choosing a negative film. The difference in graininess between films of different ISO ratings is much more pronounced in slides, so it is more important to know what is the slowest film you can use for a picture – unless, of course, you want to use grain for effect. Most photographers use slide films rated at ISO 100 or slower, in order to get high quality results. Kodachrome 64 is one particularly popular choice, but it has rather high contrast that sometimes causes highlights to be burnt-out. Fuji Velvia is a better alternative, but its ISO 50 speed rating makes it somewhat limited. A film more appropriate to portraiture is Fujichrome 100, which has a natural tendency to give warm skin tones without extra filters or gold reflectors. For more neutral results, Agfachrome 100 is a good choice, and has the benefit of giving results nearly as good when it is pushed to ISO 200, instead of the normal ISO 100.

Scotch, Fuji, and Kodak, all make higher speed films for use in poor light. They are all designed for push processing and offer very bright colours because of their high contrast. Agfa and Scotch, however, both have ISO 1000 films which have low contrast and which are great for moody shots with pastel colours.

B/W films

Black and white films offer the greatest variety of all the normal types of film. They range from ultra fine grain, in Kodak Technical Pan, to very high speed films for use in the dimmest of lighting conditions, led by the excellent Kodak T-MAX P3200. Between these extremes, are the more routine films used for general photography. Ilford FP4 Plus, rated at ISO 125, is the traditional choice for portraiture, with Kodak T-MAX 100 being the more modern alternative. Similarly, for ISO 400 films Kodak Tri-X or Ilford HP5 are the traditional choice with Kodak T-MAX 400 and Ilford Delta 400 taking

advantage of recent improvements in film technology.

Special films

There is a large number of special films, but four groups are of special relevance to portraiture.

●Ilford XP2 is a special black and white film that can be processed in colour chemicals (including mini-labs) to give black and white prints. It can also be printed on normal black and white paper for top quality results.

●Tungsten films (Scotch 640T and Kodak Ektachrome 160T) are designed to give natural colours under tungsten lighting, without having to use filters.

●Kodak 35mm infra-red films (colour slides or b/w prints) can be used for special effects. The black and white version is easier to use and process, and gives more dramatic results.

●Polaroid 35mm instant films are supplied in normal cassettes, and come with their own chemical processing packs. A special daylight tank enables film to be ready for viewing in a minute or so. Colour and b/w types are available – all are for slides. The films give pictures which are quite unlike any other, but they are rather expensive, and their very shiny surfaces may cause exposure errors with off-the-film metering systems.

2: LIGHTING AND EXPOSURE

INTRODUCTION

There is a difference between there being enough light to take a picture and there being the right lighting to take a good picture. Photographic lighting is all about manipulating light to produce a desired effect. In this chapter, we aim to explain some of the theories and techniques used in lighting for portraiture. The discussion will be kept general here; detailed lighting arrangements will be set out in later chapters where appropriate.

LOOKING AT LIGHTING

Rather than starting from described effects, you will get a better appreciation of lighting if you investigate it for yourself. The easiest way to do this is with the help of a darkened room, a powerful torch and a willing assistant to act as a model. Shine the torch on your assistant and note the effect of moving it in all directions. By varying the position of the torch, both in terms of angle around the head and distance away, you will see the various results possible. Held under the chin, the torch shows a ghoulish effect, much beloved by children at Hallowe'en but not useful for flattering portraits. A high light accentuates the forehead, and is therefore better avoided with balding men. On the other hand it also gives good modelling under cheek bones, so can be very effective for people with strong features.

LIGHTING CONTRAST

Using the torch alone tends to give stark results, with dark shadows in unlit areas. This is particularly true if the torch is held close to the subject.

This picture was taken using both on-camera flash and the tungsten light used to keep the chicks warm. It was a posed shot, which followed several less successful candid attempts.

Moving the torch further back tends to reduce the brightness of light areas, and therefore makes the darkness of the shadows appear less. You can achieve the same thing by keeping the torch close, but lightening the room. This will lighten the shadows without changing the bright areas very much, but the finished result looks similar because the lighting looks more even. Both these methods change the lighting contrast, which means that they change the relative brightnesses of the shadow areas and the light areas. The concept of lighting contrast is very important, and by understanding it you will have the most powerful tool for successful photographic lighting.

Lighting contrast needs to be considered in conjunction with the contrast of the subject, and with that of the film in use, since the final photographic effect is a combination of all three factors. So if high contrast is a problem, and the cause of the high contrast cannot be reduced, then it may be possible to reduce the contrast of the other factors in compensation. This is quite a difficult concept, because although photographers are used to thinking about light in terms of intensity, they are often less accustomed to the importance of contrast.

AN EXAMPLE OF LIGHTING CONTRAST

As an example, consider a very simplified situation in which you want to photograph a piece of card having three areas, coloured grey, black and white. You have the choice of photographing it in direct sunlight, or under the shade of a tree. Obviously there is less light under the tree, but that is not the only difference. If you had an exposure meter which could take spot readings, you might find that the exposure for the grey area of card required three stops more under the shade of the tree than it would in bright sunlight. But you would also find that in direct sunlight the difference between the brightness of the white and black areas of the card might be five or six stops, whereas under the tree it would be reduced to four stops.

Although it is not usual to photograph pieces of card, the same effect causes a very common problem in outdoor portraits. If the lighting is by direct sunlight with the sun high in the sky, dark shadows will be seen in eye sockets and under the nose and chin. The problem would be less acute if the portrait could be taken in diffused lighting in the shade, because the difference in brightness between highlights

It is obvious from the shadows on the ground that the lighting here is very harsh. In order to produce a flattering group portrait, reflectors and absorbers are being positioned to modify the lighting. The photograph was taken during a workshop held by Laurie Sands at the Fuji School Of Professional Photography.

and shadows would be less. You can also reduce the contrast by lighting the shadows and we shall be talking about techniques for doing this later in the chapter.

THE MAIN LIGHT

The prime rule of all photography is that there is always one, and only one, main light. Without this light, the subject would be very dimly lit, if at all. It determines the correct exposure, and also goes a long way towards setting the style of the photograph. Out of doors, the main light is usually the sun; indoors it is often a flashgun, and in the studio it can be any one of a variety of different light sources.

The main light can be placed anywhere around the subject, depending on the effect you want. It can be positioned in front, behind, to the left or to the right of your subject, and at, above or below eye level. Back in the days of the box camera the usual advice was to stand facing your subject with the sun coming from over your shoulder. This is good safe advice that is very often applied to other light sources. Even though there is an enormous range of possible positions, the main light is usually placed slightly to one side, towards the front, and above eye level.

In the studio, you have a good deal of control. In fact in some ways there are almost too many possible ways of setting the lighting, so a few basic arrangements have become standard starting points. One of the classic positions for the main light is directly in front of the subject and above eye level. This produces the effect known as "butterfly lighting", so called because of the shape of the nose shadow cast above the top lip. Another classic effect, known as "Rembrandt lighting", involves having the main light further to the side, and allowing one side of the face to go into shadow except for a triangular area lighting the eye, (see Chapter 5).

One of the most attractive lighting effects is that from a softly lit window. All it requires is a window, with no direct sunlight, preferably facing north. Net curtains help to soften the effect, and anybody standing close to the window is lit by a beautifully gentle light. The only usual problem is that a standard window may face towards a light outdoors, but the other side is a dark interior and the light tends to fall off very quickly as you move away from the window itself. This means that the shadow side of the face tends to be rather too dark, and a fill-in light is needed to lighten it.

FILL-IN LIGHT

Fill-in light is used to lighten shadows caused by the main light. The problem is how much lightening is required? Firstly, it is important to realise that the fill-in light must always be less bright than the main light, so that it does not affect the brightest areas. This fixes the maximum limit for the fill-in light's intensity, and in fact it is usually set one or two f-stops below this. For example, if you are using flash to fill-in the shadows caused by a bright sunny day, the areas in shadow from the sun will be lightened by flash so that they are only one or two stops less bright than the sunlit areas. This means that there will be a moderate difference in brightnesses, and detail will not be lost in deep shadows.

Fill-in light is usually provided by either a hand-held flashgun or a reflector. Which you choose depends partly on the quality of your main light. In the above example, flash

The black and white picture shows how the lights were set up to produce soft butterfly lighting. The main light was an overhead soft box, with the other light acting as a secondary light on the background. The reflector, held horizontally at chest height, serves to lighten the shadows cast by the main light. The red stripe in the final picture was a fluorescent tube which the other lights were balanced to match in terms of brightness.

In the bottom picture, a large white reflector has been put in place to lighten the nose shadow. Both pictures were taken with a Mamiya RB67 using a Polaroid back.

was used to fill-in for the sun. The harshness of the light from the flash matched that of bright sunlight. If your main light was a softer window light, it would be more appropriate to use a reflector to fill-in, to keep the overall effect soft.

Using reflectors to fill-in

A major advantage of using reflectors to fill-in is that you can see their effect and, because they are easy to move,

you can adjust them to reduce a particular shadow. By moving them closer or farther away from your model, you can choose how much contrast you leave in your picture.

Reflectors are very good for close-up portraits. When used with window lighting, they should be as close to the model as possible, without being in the picture. Outside, they can be slightly further away, but not so far as to become ineffective. This is especially true of white, and to a lesser extent gold, types. Reflectors are not generally used for larger groups, since they are unable to provide even illumination over wide areas. Also, there are times when the position of the main light means that it cannot easily be reflected to reduce the shadows. Fill-in flash, despite its different light quality, is nearly always used in these cases.

Using flash to fill-in

You cannot see the effect flash will have with your naked eye, so you need a way of working out how much flash to use. This is especially important when mixing flash with daylight, because the effect of the sunlight is very easy to see, and by adding flash you actually risk ruining the picture without knowing it.

It is a well-established rule of

28

thumb that the correct exposure for bright sunlight, is f/16 when the shutter speed is set to the same as the film ISO speed. It is also convenient that most people use ISO 100 film in bright conditions, and that many cameras have their flash synchronisation speed at 1/125 second. Given these conditions, the correct way to use fill-in flash is to set the flashgun to one or two stops wider than the lens – in this case f/11 or f/8. Choosing which of the two settings to use is a matter of trial and error. In general, a one-stop difference is better for transparency films and very light-skinned people, whereas for negative films and darker skin colours, you can often get away with a two-stop difference. If you have automatic fill-in provided by your flashgun, this choice will probably have been made for you.

One of the problems that sometimes occurs with fill-in flash is that the flashgun is simply not powerful enough. Many portraits are taken at a range of 2 metres or more, and this means that if f/11 is being set for an ISO 100 film, then the flashgun needs a guide number of at least 22. This is quite close to the limit of many cheaper flashguns, and does not even allow for the fact that flashguns are less effective out of doors because they usually rely on additional bounced light from walls and ceilings. Fortunately, fill-in flash is better underdone than overdone, so if your flash is too weak, it will probably not ruin the picture. But it is as well to bear in mind the limitations of your own flashgun.

Another problem is that many cameras' flash synchronisation speeds are a lot slower than the shutter speeds you would normally want to use in bright sunlight. But it is very important not to exceed the flash speed if the flash is to register on the whole of the picture. The problem is most likely with high-speed films, such as those with ISO ratings of 400 or more. The usual f/16 rule would suggest a shutter speed of 1/500 second, but this is faster than the usual flash synchronisation speed. It is possible to use the reciprocity rule to reduce the shutter speed, whilst making the aperture smaller, but that too is limited. The smallest aperture for many 35mm camera lenses is f/22, so it is only possible to drop the shutter speed by one f-stop, to 1/250 second. This may still be too fast to allow flash synchronisation, although many more recent cameras can synchronise with flash at this speed.

If you need to drop the shutter speed even further, fit a neutral density filter over the lens, to reduce the amount of light entering it. A polarizing filter can double-up as a neutral density filter, reducing the light by about one and a half stops. This would let you use 1/125, or even 1/60 second shutter speeds. But if you do use a filter, remember it will reduce the flash as well, so set the flashgun to one stop more powerful than you would otherwise have done. This, in turn, may take you beyond the limits of your flashgun, in which case you could move the flashgun closer to your subject. As long as the flashgun is connected to the camera by using a cable, there is no need to move the camera as well.

SECONDARY LIGHT SOURCES

A secondary light source is any light that is not the main light. They are called 'secondary' to emphasise the fact that they must always be dominated by the main light, and must never be allowed to overpower it. Fill-in lights are a particular kind of secondary light used to deal with high contrast, but there are many other cases where additional lighting is used to modify the effect of the main light.

As well as being used to fill-in shadows, secondary lights can be used to light areas completely unlit by the main light. The exact positions of secondary lights depend very much on the effect required, but common uses are to illuminate the background, or provide hair lighting. These additional lights are frequently thought of as belonging to studio set-ups, but they can be used outside as well. For example, several flashguns could be used at once, with cables or slave triggers to make them all fire at the right moment. You will often need a flash meter to get the balance right, though this applies whenever several flashguns are used.

EXPOSURE BASICS

Exposure is all about getting the image seen through the lens recorded onto film. To the

Getting the exposure right was difficult here. The chapel itself was very dark, with bright shafts of sunlight coming in through the windows. A spot meter was used to take localised readings from the sunlit areas before the couple turned to walk down the aisle. The camera was then preset to these readings and the photographer waited for the right moment.

According to the built-in camera meter, this picture was overexposed, but the meter was confused by the brightness of the snow and sky.

casual glance, exposure is very simple, but it can get very complicated. A basic concept is the idea of an 18% grey subject, and it is to this that most meters are calibrated. The theory is that if all the lightnesses and darknesses in a typical picture were to be averaged out, the result would be an 18% grey tone. It is then a simple matter to calibrate exposure meters so that the 18% grey scene gives a fixed,

preset negative density. All areas which are lighter or darker than this are recorded with correspondingly denser or thinner areas of negative. It is this principle which is used in basic built-in camera meters, and which produces correctly exposed pictures under most circumstances.

But what happens when the scene does not average to 18% grey, or when the contrast level is too high for the film to record? In both these cases, you need to decide what is the most important part of the picture, and to set the exposure appropriate to that area. Many high technology cameras can do this, but their interpretation of the most important part may not be the same as yours. Also, they do not know how light or dark those areas should be, and so they still have to resort to the 18% grey reference.

Exposure for skin colour
Suppose you want to take a portrait of two people, one dark skinned and the other fair skinned. You want to do very tight headshots of each individually, and also a shot of the two together. The pictures are to be done outdoors, on a hazy day with soft lighting. Framing the fair-skinned person first, using a 135mm or similar lens, your camera's built in meter tells you that it

requires 1/250 sec at f/8. You take the photograph then frame up on the second person, and the meter recommends 1/125 sec at f/5.6 in this case. That done, you go on to set up the group photo, but even before you check the meter reading, you suspect you may have problems, because the individual pictures required different exposures, so how can you have a single exposure for the pair? In fact, the camera meter would probably suggest 1/250 sec, at something between f/8 and f/5.6.

Average European skin tones are remarkably close to the 18% grey standard, so the exposure recommended for the fair-skinned person is likely to be correct. But the camera's meter assumes that the second person still has 18% grey tone skin, as it can't know that the skin is actually darker. It attributes the darker reading to a lower light level and so recommends extra exposure. This will make the skin look too fair, and could result in the background becoming burnt-out. Going back to the group shot, the background will probably average to 18% grey, and the reduced relative size of the people's heads will mean the exposure is less influenced by them.

The safest solution is to make sure that all your light readings used for setting the exposure are based on a very definite 18% grey subject. Kodak manufacture a card which has a surface that is an exact 18% grey reflector, so any light reading taken from this card will be accurate, provided that the card is lit by the same light as the subject you intend to photograph. If you had used the grey card in the example of the two people, you would have realised that there was just one exposure which was correct for all three pictures.

Other metering systems

Another way of metering a scene, without being influenced by the tone of the subject, is to use incident light readings. This is done using a hand-held meter, most commonly one of the Weston series, fitted with a diffusing cone – called an 'Invercone'. The meter is held close to the subject, but pointing towards the camera position. This gives a measure of how much light is falling onto the subject when viewed from the camera angle. Incident light measurement is therefore a fool proof way of measuring the light and it is also the only reliable method for metering flash. You need a special flash meter to measure the intensity of a short flash burst, but the method for using it is exactly the same as for a normal incident light meter. Combined flash and daylight meters are available, but they tend to be very expensive compared to a second-hand Weston meter and a separate basic flash meter.

Spot meters

Spot meters enable you to meter a very small area, a distant face, for example. This is useful when you just cannot get close to your subject, such as when taking candid or celebrity pictures. Spot meters are also commonly used to determine contrast. You can take exposure readings from shadow and highlight areas, and it is the ratio between these readings which indicates the contrast. If there is too much contrast for the film to handle, you can revise the exposure to be certain of retaining either shadow or highlight detail – depending on which is the more important. If the highlights are important, you should underexpose the film relative to the 18% grey exposure. The reverse is true if shadow detail is more important, although tradition has it that you should always expose negatives for the shadows, and give whatever development is appropriate to the highlights. Unfortunately, this advice cannot be used for colour negative films because they are all designed to be given standard development times. You should therefore

remember to think about the shadows and highlights when you actually take the picture.

Deviating from the correct exposure

The correct exposure is one which records tones, so that your picture looks as bright as the original scene, but this may not always be the overriding consideration. One common reason for deviating from the correct exposure is to get better colour saturation in colour transparencies. You can do this by setting the exposure to half a stop less than the correct metered setting. Similarly, colour print film tends to have better colours if it is overexposed – usually by about one stop. Black and white film is usually given the very minimum exposure, because this also minimises the grain size. Kodak T-MAX 400 is actually advertised for its ability to be under-exposed without loss of quality, so it makes sense to rate this film at ISO 800 all the time.

Effect of coloured lighting

You need to be careful when metering light which is not the same colour as daylight. Either the light itself may be a different colour, such as the yellowish colour of tungsten lamps, or the light may be filtered – including the use of filters over the camera lens if

This picture was taken in a theatre under tungsten stage lighting, so an extra stop of exposure was allowed to compensate for the meter's daylight calibration.

an inbuilt meter is being used. In all these cases the light does not have the same spectral quality as the daylight for which the meter was calibrated. The result is that the meter reading may be inaccurate, and it is for this reason that filters are given filter factors. These factors should be used to revise the unfiltered light reading, and so avoid any possible inaccuracy in exposure. This is most important with more densely coloured filters, and in the extreme case of the Kodak Wratten infra-red 87 filter, the error caused by relying on auto exposure with the filter in place is five stops – enough to ruin the photograph completely. Using daylight meters under tungsten studio lighting gives about 1 to 1½ stops of underexposure, so allow more exposure than the meter suggests.

3: COMPOSITION AND POSING

INTRODUCTION

Composition is about how things are arranged within the frame, posing is how the subjects are arranged within the composition. In this chapter, we will look at composition first, then posing.

COMPOSITION

The photographer's job is to compose the photograph so that the important details are highlighted and nothing is given undue emphasis in the photograph unless it contributes to the overall effect. When we view the world, our eyes automatically pick out what is important in a scene and ignore what is irrelevant. A photograph is a two dimensional representation of a part of that three dimensional scene. A camera is unselective; it cannot choose to ignore details as our eyes can. For example, people looking at a child playing in the park might see the child's absorbed expression and the warmth of the afternoon light. A photograph of the same scene could highlight brightly coloured crisp packets that litter the sandpit. It might lose impact by including other people who are nothing to do with the child, and who would be ignored by anyone watching.

The first thing to do is to visualise the finished picture and to think about what effect you want to create. You may have to do this very quickly, but a second's thought can make all the difference. You need to decide where to place your subject or subjects within the frame of the picture. How big should they appear? Is this going to be a tight head shot? How much background do you want to include and how obvious should it be? What do you want the viewer to notice first in the photograph?

Methods of composing a photograph

There are a number of different techniques you can use to compose your picture. We shall be looking at several standard methods of composition here. The first method is to look at how things are arranged within the plane of the photograph, i.e. how you use the position of the subject to guide your viewers' eyes.

Imagine your picture is divided into thirds, both horizontally and vertically by two sets of lines. Artists discovered long ago that the eye is drawn to anything that lies on any of these imaginary lines, and anything that lies on the four intersections is especially noticeable. This is known as the 'rule of thirds'.

This picture is a classic example of rule of thirds composition. William Frost, who campaigned to protect park trees, is placed on a vertical third; his dog is on a horizontal third as is the distant horizon. The picture won a Kodak Press Award for Jon Tarrant.

Portraits are very often taken so that the subject's eyes lie on one of the lines or intersections. A standard head and shoulders shot, for example, could have the eyes a third of the way down the picture. This tends to leave a small gap between the top of the head and the top of the picture and a reasonable amount of shoulder at the bottom. The overall effect is pleasing and balanced. If you want to take a fuller length picture of someone against a background, you might use a horizontal format with your model positioned one third of the way in from the side of the picture. In this way you can include a lot of background detail, and yet the subject is still dominant.

You can also guide the viewer's eyes by using a frame within the frame of the picture. Trees, doors, arches and so on can be used on location. Sometimes the frame itself may suggest a good idea for a portrait. In a studio, framing can also be done with the lighting. The light is strongest around the subject and falls away so the background is less bright. You can achieve something of this effect on location by using vignettes.

The line of the road stretching into the distance emphasises the child's isolation.

The entire effect, here, relies on saturated complementary colours. The picture was taken in a small, dimly lit, pub rock venue. The film used was Scotch P800/3200 rated at ISO 1600 in order to avoid using flash, which would have destroyed the atmosphere.

Geometric lines are another useful device, and can be used to point out the principle subject. For example, in a picture of a child sitting in the middle of a roundabout, the handles dividing the roundabout into sectors converge at the centre and lead the eye towards the child. You should always be aware of strong, geometric lines in your picture. Any that do not add anything specifically, tend to distract and weaken the overall effect.

Another method of composition is to look at the tones, colours and textures of the various elements of your picture. You can put similar elements together, or juxtapose unlike elements to emphasise the contrast between them. So, for example, you could compose a picture around pastel or very strong colours, or you could make a strong colour stand out by being surrounded by more muted hues. If you wanted to give an impression of someone bathed in a warm light, you could heighten the effect by using golden tones in the lighting, the model's clothes and the background. Texture can often be used to give a feeling of opulence, with materials like velvet, or starkness, using concrete or hard, modern furniture.

Having decided what is going to be the main thrust of your composition, there's nothing to stop your using other methods as well so that your picture is as cohesive as possible.

Backgrounds

Be very aware of the background. If it is cluttered, try to clear it. Move objects such as furniture and litter, or move yourself and your model away from the distractions. You can often hide things you don't want in the picture behind the model. Exactly what will draw the viewer's attention away from the subject depends on whether you are shooting in black and white or colour. For colour pictures, watch out for items whose colour stands out – red objects, no matter how small, tend to attract attention. With black and white, tone, shape and texture are more important. Something red might not be obvious, but a kite tangled in a tree stands out because of its shape. Using narrow depth of field and focusing sharply on your subject, helps reduce the effect of distracting backgrounds. Sometimes, you may also have the option of control in the darkroom to make the background more pleasing, but in all cases it is better to try to remove distracting elements, than to have to disguise them later.

Don't forget you can usually move yourself, as well as your subject. If you possibly can, take the opportunity to explore your location before you do the shoot. You may see a good place to take a portrait, but discover an even better one by moving only a few feet. It is important to have a clear idea of what you want before you start, and to avoid taking your models on a ten mile hike. But allow yourself the flexibility to ask them to move to take advantage of a shaft of sunlight for example.

Props

Think carefully about what you include in the picture, as well as what you exclude. You can use props to suggest something about the person or people you are photographing. Props can be very elaborate, but often simplicity gets you better results. A simple prop, such as an elderly man's pipe, can say a great deal about the sitter, as can a musician's violin. The most important thing about props is that they contribute to the picture as a whole. Do not use them merely as space fillers. A chair is one of the most useful props. Models are often much more relaxed sitting down, particularly if they are not used to having their picture taken. But think about what kind of chair you want to use. If you want a

picture of someone looking comfortable, try an armchair or an upholstered sofa. For elegance, you could drape your subject over a chaise longue. Try to keep your props in harmony with your background. A kitchen stool would look out of place in a 'Homes and Garden' drawing room.

POSING

The typical passport picture of someone sitting square-on to the camera and staring blankly into the lens is a classic example of a bad portrait. It is bad because, although a passport picture shows you what someone *looks* like, it shows nothing of what the person *is* like. When you pose a model, what you are effectively trying to do is to give an impression of personality as it comes through his or her body language. This means expressing age, sex, sexuality, mood and so on through the pose.

Cropping

First of all, you need to decide how much of your model you want to show. This can range from a tight head shot that

Although this picture looks posed, it was taken in a split second as the child became aware of the photographer.

shows only the main facial features (there are even portraits that just show someone's eyes), to a shot with a lot of background and where the model is quite small in the picture.

There are some standard places to crop a picture, which give a pleasing effect. Perhaps more important, cropping straight across joints tends to look awkward. So try to include all the shoulders for a head and shoulders shot, for example. A half-length shot is generally cropped at the waist and a three-quarter length from mid-thigh to just above the knee. Cutting across the knee looks most peculiar, and never crop the ankles in what is composed to be a full length shot.

Establishing a relationship

It is important for you to establish a rapport with your sitters. You need to give them confidence in you as a photographer and themselves as models. (We are assuming that you will be taking pictures almost entirely of amateur models.) A lot of people do not like having their picture taken, and most are nervous in front of a camera.

Get as much as possible done before you start posing your model. This will make the process less boring for your sitters and you will look as though you know what you are doing. Have your camera set up, the background arranged, and work out exactly how you are going to pose your sitter for at least the first few shots. You should also have in mind other poses for later. This allows you to concentrate on your subject as much as possible, rather than on your equipment. If you do need to alter your set-up, explain what you are doing, in plain language rather than technical jargon, and allow your model to drop the pose.

Establish a relationship quickly. All this means is being friendly and chatty. This should be easy with family and friends, but even they may react differently to you when you are in your role as photographer. Explain what you want to do and how long it will take. If you are setting up the shoot yourself, you can do this in a meeting or telephone call beforehand, so your model will know what to expect before you start.

Try to stick to your stated brief. If you experiment without explaining, your model will lose confidence in you and start to get nervous. However, if you suddenly have an idea for a marvellous shot, stop, tell your model what the idea is and ask if it is alright to carry on for a while longer. Be prepared to take 'no' for an answer.

Not only are people placed left to right, but also top to bottom. This makes good use of the negative area and the location, and the result is much more interesting than everyone standing in a straight line.

Do not wait for the perfect expression before pressing the shutter. Once the session is under-way, your sitter will start to relax. Film is cheap, and it is worth wasting a few frames to put him or her at ease.

Be reassuring. When things are right, tell your sitter. If they are wrong, ask him or her to change, without criticising.

Never blame the model. You, the photographer, are responsible for how the picture turns out.

Positioning the head
Before you pose your model, you have to make a number of decisions about what you are trying to show. Do you want to flatter your model, so that he

43

Two different moods were achieved by using a tight head shot and a head and shoulders composition. The lighting, clothes and background added to the effects.

or she looks as attractive as possible? Or do you want to bring out the facial features as they really are? Is there a particular mood you are trying to capture?

A classical pose for a head and shoulders portrait is with the model's shoulders on a diagonal to the camera and the head turned to give a three-quarter view. This gives lots of eye contact and a flattering shape to the face and the neck. However, if the head is turned too far, the neck can become wrinkled.

Full face portraits suggest power and sexiness because the eye contact is very direct. These are excellent for assertive sitters with strong expressions. Try using a full-face portrait if you want to show someone laughing or in a rage, for example. You can emphasise striking features by taking a very tight, full-face head shot. This can work particularly well with old people, whose faces are full of detail.

Profiles are tricky. Most people are not used to seeing themselves in profile and they may become self conscious. Also, because there is little eye contact, it is difficult to get a natural looking pose. On the other hand, profiles can help to produce stunningly stylish portraits – especially as silhouettes.

Remember that there is a whole range of views between

profile and full-face. It is easy to experiment with the position of the head, because you only have to ask your model to move a small amount to get another view. The only position to avoid is between profile and three-quarter, where the nose breaks the line of the cheek. This gives a very unpleasing effect.

The tilt of the head can also say a lot and, in particular, can be used to flatter. Tilting the head down slightly strengthens the jaw line and lengthens the face. If the head is tilted further, it can lead to a menacing expression, so be careful if all you want to do is give the face a clean shape. Conversely, tilting the head up gives an effect of innocence or reflection. You can often see this in old Hollywood style portraits, where an almost childlike effect is created by a woman gazing upwards with wide eyes, emphasising the round babyishness of her face. Camera angle is important here. The neutral position is to keep it at normal eye level, but to exaggerate the effect of tilting the head, move your camera in the opposite direction.

Match the position of the head with the direction of the eyes. Moving the eyes towards or away from the camera has far more effect on the finished picture then moving the head. Regardless of how the head is

Poses looking upwards have a lighter feel than soulful downcast eyes.

angled, a photograph with the eyes looking upwards is lighter than one where the eyes look down. So the maximum impact you can get is a full-face shot with the model looking straight into the middle of the lens. However, it can be disconcerting to the model to be faced with the camera staring straight back. Very often your model will find it easier to look at the top or bottom edge of the lens. During a shoot, it is more comfortable for the model if you start off with poses looking less directly towards the camera, saving the most challenging shots until later.

Positioning the hands
If you want to show hands in a portrait, use them to add to the overall effect. There are standard positions for hands that everyone recognises as meaning certain things. This goes deeper than the obvious fist for aggression. For example, hands folded over one another indicate trust, as can be seen in a lot of portraits of politicians. Clasped hands with the fingers interlinked look assertive, but can be distracting and untidy.

People often don't know what to do with their hands. A natural and comfortable pose is with the face resting on the hands. However, be careful to ask your model not to rest too firmly, unless you want a fed-up look. Shaping the fingers gently round the face looks pleasing.

Beware of awkward hands dangling by people's sides when you take full length, standing portraits. Even worse is the macho man who clasps his hands over his groin – very defensive. A standard pose is to put one hand in a pocket and rest the other against the thigh, with the leg slightly fowards. You can also use a pocket to hook the thumb with the fingers straight out or curved. Having both hands in the pockets is reminiscent of the thirties, when baggy trousers made this more comfortable. Today it tends to look old-fashioned.

People often use their hands very expressively when they speak. Try getting your model to talk about something interesting whilst you take pictures. You can get highly animated and exciting portraits like this. But pictures of people talking need to be timed very carefully, as catching people with their mouth wide open in mid-sentence can make them look gormless.

Positioning the body
It is essential that all the various parts of your sitter's body look as though they belong together. Legs and arms should look like pairs, so don't let them hang any old how. People often slouch in front of a camera with their legs slightly apart and their

Even numbered groups are difficult to pose, because the symmetry tends to produce boring results. By converting two individuals into one couple, using head angles and pose, the photographer has produced a very loving portrait.

toes turned in. This looks disjointed and gawky. Props really come into their own here as people find it much easier to get into a natural position if they have something to sit on or lean against.

Be very wary of limbs positioned straight towards the camera. Arms and legs become distorted and start to dominate the picture. In particular, men have a tendency to sit with a wide leg cross. If the crossed foot is nearest to the camera, it will appear to be much larger than it really is.

Explore different shapes, such as curves and triangles, and use arms and legs to emphasise them. Even without asking your model to be a gymnast, you can experiment with posing the body in all sorts of ways.

Camera angle
You can add to the effectiveness of your model's pose by the camera angle you choose. To flatter women, have your camera angled fairly high. This emphasises the hair and the eyes open wider when

looking up towards the camera. There is a double effect on the neck in that the pose tends to stretch it, making it look longer and more elegant, but too high a camera angle will cause the neck to be hidden by the head and so appear shorter.

It is more usual to flatter men by holding the camera at chest height, giving the model an impression of dignity and height. A low camera angle also reduces any bald areas and gives the impression of a strong jaw. However, it can also emphasise a double chin, which is not likely to please anyone.

The higher or lower the camera angle, the more dramatic the impact. You can get effective head-only shots with high angles, perhaps making the body out of focus or very dark. Menace and power are added to a picture, as the camera angle drops and the bulk of the body starts to dominate the picture.

Groups

When you are posing groups, it is important to remember why you have chosen to take this particular set of people together. Use the relationships within the group to build up your picture. Arrange your group in general first, before worrying about the details of each individual's pose.

One of the most boring ways of taking a group portrait is to line everybody up and then mow them down. It is far more interesting to have people's heads on different levels. You can do this in a variety of ways; having some people kneeling, some standing and some sitting; using boxes, chairs – even telephone books, as long as they do not intrude into the picture – for people to stand or sit on. You can also pose people on a slope or a flight of stairs. However, be careful not to have too much space between people's eye lines, or the group may look disjointed.

We perceive those on a higher level or at the centre of attention as having more authority. So if your group has a natural leader, such as the boss or the team captain, you can place him or her at the highest point in the picture or right in the middle of the group. You may find it easier to position the leader first, then bring in everyone else. If you don't want to give too rigid a picture of levels of authority, you can use the rule of thirds (see page 36), so that the leader is in a commanding position within the picture, but not necessarily at the top.

Once you have your group basically sorted out, you can attend to details. Groups will often have props that show what binds them together. This can be the equipment a hobby group might use, or the tools of trade for some workers. You can use these props to direct your viewer's eyes to important details, particularly if there are a lot of straight lines. Oars or fishing rods, for example, could be held by the outside members of a team and used to frame the group.

You can also make a group look more cohesive by using people's body language. In general, if people belong together, they tend to sit or stand so they are turned towards their companions. Ask your sitters to turn their shoulders if they're standing, or their knees if sitting. Get them to put an arm around the person next to them if this is appropriate, especially with family groups. Small children can be sat on someone's knee, which also introduces another convenient eye level.

Two can often be a difficult number to pose. A standard pose, especially for a man and a woman, is for one person's eyes to be on a level with the other's mouth. However, this makes the top person appear much more dominant. If you do not want to give such a strong sense of hierarchy, but are worried about having two pairs of eyes on the same level, try experimenting with where

This tightly posed group was taken with a wide angle lens from a high angle. The lighting was harsh and all the women are looking directly into the camera. These factors add to the power of the picture, which was a production publicity shot.

people are looking. For example, you could ask a couple to lean their heads together and look at each other out of the corners of their eyes. Or one person could lean over the other's shoulder.

Finally, a word about format. Group photos are often seen as being horizontal shots, but it is worth thinking about positioning your group to suit a vertical format. This is particularly true for small groups or couples.

4: THE HOME STUDIO

INTRODUCTION

Portraits are often automatically associated with the photographic studio. This means that when people start to take portraiture seriously, they tend to think they need access to professional facilities. This is not true. Firstly, very few types of portraiture really need a studio, and secondly, even when a studio is required it can be very basic. In fact, all a studio needs to be is a clear space in which to take photographs. This chapter is about setting up a studio at home in an ordinary living room with the minimum of fuss and expense.

ROOM SIZE, AND LENS FOCAL LENGTH

The most common cause of difficulties in home studios is trying to do too much in too little space. In chapter 1, we said that head and shoulder portraits are best suited to lenses of about 90mm focal length. This means the camera needs to be about five feet away from the model. There should also be two or three feet of space behind the model, and four or five feet behind the camera, so you will need a room some twelve feet long even for tightly-framed portraits.

Many photographers switch to a standard, or even a wide-angle, lens for fuller length shots to get more into the picture. This actually makes matters worse. The problem is the difference in distances between the camera and the closest and furthest parts of the model – and how this affects perspective. The nose is about five or six inches closer to the camera than the ears, and it is important that this difference in distance should be small compared to the camera to subject distance. You need to be particularly aware of this for headshots, where the camera is close to the model. Using the 90mm lens at a range of five feet, means the five or six inch difference is only one twelfth of the total distance, and the resulting photograph looks natural. If, on the other hand, a head and shoulders picture was framed with a 28mm lens, the camera would be only just over a foot away from the model, and the difference would be almost half as much again. The face would seem to bulge towards the camera in a most unflattering way.

The same is true if the camera is positioned further back, in an attempt to photograph a full-length pose. Assuming the camera is at about waist height, a 28mm lens will mean the camera being seven feet away from the model. Although this fits nicely

Sitting the child on a rocking horse kept him still enough for the picture to be taken, and interested enough for him to have a happy expression. Lighting on the child has been balanced with the brightness of the window so that the detail on the window can still be seen. Photographed on Fuji Reala 120 roll film, courtesy of Fuji Photo Film (UK) Ltd.

| Lens focal length | Camera to subject distances required for | |
	Head and shoulders	**Half length**
50 mm	2–3 feet	4–6 feet
90 mm	5 feet	8 feet
135 mm	7 feet	10 feet

into a large living room, the wide angle of view introduces exactly the same type of distortion which gives the bulging face in close-up. The net result is a photograph where technical quality and flattering the model have been sacrificed for the sake of getting more in. Where space is limited, it is much better to accept the restrictions before you start, and to plan your pictures accordingly.

BACKGROUNDS

Another factor which controls the kind of pictures you can do in a temporary studio is the background. Photographs which have ordinary room backgrounds always look as if they were taken in ordinary rooms – to give a studio feel the background needs to be more controlled. Very occasionally, a plain painted wall is suitable, but more often it is necessary to introduce a special photographic background.

In a professional studio, backgrounds are provided by large rolls of plain paper in a variety of colours. There is no reason why you shouldn't buy a background roll and set it up at home, but it can work out to be very expensive. A much cheaper and easier alternative is to use plain material. Sheets, blankets, or plain curtains could all be suitable and are readily available. Sheets are particularly convenient because their light weight makes them easy to suspend from a ceiling, or drape over a string fixed to the walls. Old sheets are every bit as useable as new ones, and it doesn't matter if they are slightly tatty, as long as obvious flaws do not show in the picture. They can also be dyed easily, either all one colour or to give an abstract coloured pattern. But if you do go for a pattern, remember that it must not distract from the subject, so you should avoid small dots, hard lines and recognisable shapes – unless they are there for a deliberate effect.

LIGHTING

Lighting a home studio is a potential minefield. It is easy to think that the more money you spend, the better your lighting will be. In practice, good lighting isn't about the equipment itself, but about how it is used. The simplest home studio requires no artificial light at all, and simply makes use of window lighting (see chapter 2), although there is no doubt that this is rather limiting.

Types of lighting

Artificial lights for photography are divided into two types; flash lighting and tungsten lamps, (which are similar to ordinary house lights but much brighter). Flash is normally thought of as more sophisticated, and therefore more in keeping with the high technology image of modern photography, whereas tungsten lighting is often regarded as old-fashioned. This is an inappropriate distinction, because both types of lighting have their advantages and disadvantages.

A guide to tungsten lighting

There are several different kinds of tungsten lamps. The two main types are photofloods, a photographic version of household light bulbs, and photographic lamps, which are particularly designed to match the quality of tungsten balanced films.

Photofloods come in two

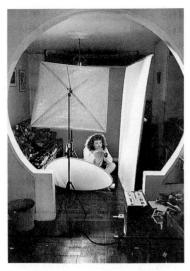

Transforming a house room into a temporary studio can be done with the minimum of fuss, provided there is enough floor space. Room ceilings are often much lower than ideal studio ceilings, so a useful hint is to sit your model on the floor, effectively increasing the height of the ceiling above the model.

sizes; the No. 1 rated at 275 watts and the No. 2 rated at 500 watts. Although they may be available in standard bayonet fittings, they are too powerful and get too hot for household light sockets. It is more common to find them with a screw-base fitting and to mount them in custom-made holders. Both sizes of bulbs

53

This picture has a very formal studio feel, but was actually taken in the bride's home using window light with a white reflector opposite.

have a very short life and a colour temperature of 3,400K.

Photographic lamps are far more useful because they have longer lives (typically about 100 hours) and because their 3,200K colour temperature exactly matches tungsten balanced film. Some bulbs have integral reflectors coated onto the bulbs themselves, but it is more useful to have a bare bulb and a variety of external reflectors from which to choose. A starter kit of tungsten lighting can cost under £100.

A guide to flash units

There are important differences between flashguns of the type meant for mounting directly onto a camera and free-standing flash units. These include size, weight, power, judging the lighting, method of controlling exposure, connection to the camera, power supply, varying the quality of the light and cost. In the case of on-camera flashguns, most of these things are hardly variable at all, or are automated. Given this lack of control, versatile flash units for the studio can seem thoroughly daunting, though this need not be the case.

Size and weight are reasonably standard. Most common flash units are about the same size as a shoe box and weigh 2–3Kg. Obviously,

more powerful units tend to be bigger and heavier. Whereas tungsten lamps are rated in watts like ordinary bulbs and portable flashguns have guide numbers, free standing flash units can be specified in either way.

The guide number system can only be applied to a single flash unit with a specific reflector attached. If you use a different reflector, even on the same flash unit, the guide number will change. The power, however, does not change, so it is more usual to use the power consumption of a flash unit in joules or watt-seconds as a guide to its light output. With most flash units, it is possible to adjust the power of the flash from full to perhaps one-sixteenth. You can control exposures by changing the flash intensity rather than changing the lens aperture. This gives you the freedom to set the aperture for depth of field, then to adjust the lights to suit. However, you need a flash meter as free-standing flash units cannot be camera controlled when it comes to exposure. Studio flash units may also be equipped with modelling lamps in each flash head, which allow you to assess the effect of your lighting arrangements before you take the picture.

One way to connect the camera to the flash unit is by

using a cable that plugs into the flash unit and into the camera's flash socket, provided it has one. The same cable can be used to connect the flash meter to the lights when checking exposures. Some flash meters do not need a cable connector, but it is often easier to use one as it means that the flashes can be fired from the meter itself.

It is not always necessary to use a cable connector between the camera and flash units. If each flash is equipped with a slave unit, all the units can be fired from a small flashgun mounted on the camera. The triggering flashgun must be dim enough not to affect the lighting and has the advantage of enabling you to reduce the number of hazardous trailing wires.

Although some flash units can be powered from car batteries, they are all designed primarily to be operated from the mains electricity supply.

One way in which flash is very different to tungsten is the degree to which the light can be modified by accessories. Because the lights keep quite cool, it is feasible to use plastic

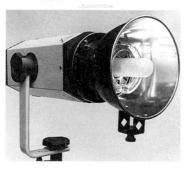

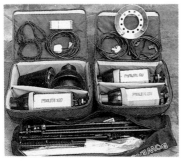

i) Front view of a free standing flash unit. (Top left)
ii) Rear view showing the control panel. (Above)
iii) A complete flash kit in three bags, containing enough equipment for most home studio and location situations. (Left)

and fabric fitments without fear of them bursting into flames. Soft boxes can be used to give a large evenly-spread light which produces soft edged shadows. Snoots and honeycombs can be used to narrow the light onto a small area, and filters can be used to change the colour of the light.

When choosing a flash unit, you should pay careful attention to the range of accessories available, as well as the requirements you may have for the flash units themselves. Even the cheapest system will cost about £100 for a single flash unit, with better models costing £200 or more. Complete flash kits generally start at about £500.

Choosing between flash and tungsten

There is clearly a very substantial price advantage in buying tungsten lighting, but this should be considered in the light of other advantages and disadvantages listed in the table. In addition, there is a rather more personal consideration – namely how the lighting feels to the photographer. This is rather like the way in which using a medium format camera feels more natural to some photographers. It is something that can only be decided by trying out both types of lighting and seeing which one

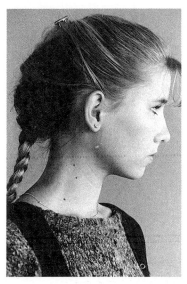

Profiles do not always make good portraits because many people are very aware of their nose and chin. In this case, however, it is a perfect success – with a whisp of hair bought forward to take advantage of the side-on pose.

you prefer. This is one area where camera clubs come into their own, not only offering first hand experience from people who own the equipment, but also providing studios and lights which you can try out yourself.

One very real difference is the quality of lighting given by flash and tungsten lights. Flash lends itself more readily to

Lighting type	Advantages	Disadvantages
Tungsten lamps	Cheap Easy to see effects Lightweight	Lamps get very hot Continuously bright Long exposures Not daylight colour
Flash lighting	Freezes motion Daylight coloured Lights stay cool Comfortable for model Compact	Relatively costly Hard to see effects

softly lit pictures, and tungsten bulbs to moody situations which make the most of shadows. One reason for this is because tungsten lighting is easier to judge by eye, whereas the low power modelling lights housed within flash units only give a rough guide as to how flash lighting will look in the finished picture. Similarly, flash softboxes are the ideal way to achieve softly-lit results. You may well find yourself more drawn to one type of lighting because it suits your style.

How many lights?
The question of how many lights you need is a difficult one, because it depends on the desired effects. The minimum, obviously, is a single light. Used with a flat reflector to fill in the shadows, this can be quite adequate for some situations; it is, after all, the situation which usually exists in outdoor sunlight. In the studio, it is very useful to have a second light which provides separation of the subject from the background, either by front lighting the background or backlighting the subject, or even both at the same time. So the comfortable minimum studio lighting kit consists of two lights and a flat reflector.

A third light to provide fill-in at the front, and a fourth to allow the background to be lit separately, may be useful sometimes. It would be very rare for a home studio to require more lighting than this. In any case, it would be sensible to buy fewer lights each with more power, than to get extra lights, because this gives you more overall flexibility in your lighting.

Only one light, bounced off a white reflector, was needed for this picture. The print was burnt in to darken the edge where the single light had spilled onto the background.

5: CHARACTER STUDIES

INTRODUCTION

Portrait photography traditionally conjures up an image of a formal character study taken in the studio. The subject is usually an old man lit with harsh side lighting to reveal every wrinkle in the skin or a glamorous young woman with flawless skin and a bland expression. The framing is tight, just head and shoulders, the background is plain and props are kept to a minimum.

But character studies are about more than that. They are about showing the personality in the face. Anyone whose face interests you, man, woman, old, young or middle-aged, is a good subject for a character study. You want someone who you feel can convey emotion. Once you have chosen your subject, you need to be very clear about what you want to bring out in your portrait. When you have decided that, you can go on to set up the lighting, background, props and pose accordingly.

The shadow under the nose gives away the classic butterfly lighting used for this picture. It is unusual in that it was taken outside and flash was used as the main light, with the sunlight providing fill-in and side hair lighting.

WHERE TO START

Since you are interested in your sitter's mood and expression, you must not allow him or her to become bored with the photography, or it is liable to show in the face. Try to set up the studio before your subject arrives. Most of the studio can be arranged quite easily, but the lighting is more difficult because it needs to be suited to the person being photographed. That said, there are two general lighting methods one of which is usually used for women and the other for men.

BUTTERFLY LIGHTING/ LIGHTING FOR WOMEN

Butterfly lighting gives a shadow under the nose like a butterfly in flight, hence its name. It can also be known as top-to-bottom lighting as the main light is directly in front of the sitter and above eye level. The shadows cast emphasise the cheekbones and minimise other features. The nose, especially, looks less prominent as the shadow is beneath, rather than to the side of it. Butterfly lighting is mostly used for women where high cheekbones and softer features are considered an advantage. Many classic photographs of Hollywood actresses are taken in this way. It is less flattering

By changing body angle, hair style and clothing, character studies can be made to look sophisticated or challenging. In particular, the very direct gaze of the right hand picture makes the model look powerful. It is surprising how much difference there is in mood, even though the head has been moved very little.

to men, as it emphasises a receding hairline.

The height of the main light determines the size of the nose shadow. The shadow looks very unflattering if it touches the top lip, and this places quite tight limits on how you position the main light. The next problem is how close the light should be to the subject. Bringing it closer means the face will be more brightly lit, and also that the shadows will be softer edged – although they will also appear darker – see chapter 2, page 24. Remember that tungsten lights can get

very hot so it is better to use flash units if you want to put the lights very close to your sitter without causing discomfort. As a guide to distance, soft lighting is usually just about within arm's reach of the sitter.

No matter how close the main light gets, or how large a light source it is, there will always be a shadow under the nose as long as the light comes from above. In very soft lighting, using soft boxes, the shadow may be sufficiently unobtrusive to be left uncorrected, but it is more common for the shadow to look too dark. It can be reduced by using a fill-in light, but you must be careful.

It is tempting to think that the fill-in light should be placed below eye level to counteract the shadows cast by the high main light. However, the only reason that shadows are visible is because the camera angle is different from the lighting angle. By placing another light at another angle you risk creating new shadows when filling-in the original ones. The correct place for the fill-in light is as close as possible to the camera angle, with the intensity adjusted to give the required degree of shadow lightening. If the fill-in light becomes so bright that it removes all shadows, then it will have become the main light, and a very flat picture will result – much like photographs taken using on-camera flash.

This is the technique of Hollywood lighting, with a high main light at the front, and a fill-in light to control shadow darkness. The modern equivalent, much used on covers of women's magazines, replaces the fill-in light with a reflector held very close under the sitter's chin. It is angled from below, but is as near as possible to the line of the camera view. There is no danger of creating new shadows when using reflectors, because they are always less bright than the light they reflect.

Sometimes it is very difficult to place a light directly above and in front of the sitter, because the light stand cuts across the picture. One way around the problem is to use a counterweighted boom arm, to hold the light horizontally with the floor stand well out of shot. Unfortunately this requires the purchase of such a boom, and a more sturdy than normal stand to take the extra weight. A simpler solution is to have the main light very slightly to the side, so that the stand is just out of view. The slight side angle of the light will start to cause side shadows on the nose, which gives the picture a stronger feel than before. If this is not required, the shadow can be moderated by placing a large white reflector on the opposite side to the light, but as close as possible to the sitter.

REMBRANDT LIGHTING/ LIGHTING FOR MEN

The classic side lighting technique is known as Rembrandt lighting, and involves having one side of the face fully-lit whilst the other is lit in just a small triangular area which includes the eye. Side lighting gives this effect naturally, provided that it is carefully positioned, because the eye socket recess allows light onto the far side of the face while the forehead and nose block it above and below. By moving the main light up or down from eye level, the lit triangle can be moved oppositely. When making such fine adjustments, it is important that the lighting is much brighter than any ambient lighting so that the effects can be seen clearly. This is where tungsten lighting comes in so useful. If you are using flash, you will probably need to shoot some Polaroid tests to see how it will look, because flash modelling lights only give a rough indication of the final result.

The definition of the nose is often a good clue to how strongly the person photographed will come across. It is no surprise, therefore, that this style of lighting is more often used for men, with defining shadows left quite dark. Sometimes there is a fill-in light or reflector opposite the main light, but one thing that is totally useless for character lighting, is to set up two lights at 45° to the subject, one to the left and the other to the right. Setting up identical lights like this is only used for copying documents, where the lighting is supposed to be flat and featureless. For character studies it is better just to use one light, or to ensure that the second light is much less powerful, or further back, than the main light.

POSING FOR CHARACTER STUDIES

Simplicity is the key to good character studies. Most people are more comfortable when they sit, so you should aim to do your pictures from seated poses. Bear this in mind when you are setting up the lighting, because eye level will be correspondingly lower than for a standing pose. High back chairs are generally to be avoided, because they intrude into the picture. Stools are also unsuitable, because some people do not feel safe on them. The best kind of chair is the wood and canvas type usually associated with movie directors, or camping. It has a medium height back, and side arms which allow some degree of flexibility in posing.

Encourage your sitter to sit as they feel comfortable, but

This is typical of Rembrandt lighting. Maximum impact is obtained when the lit area is around the eye – especially for dark-skinned models where high contrast within the eye results in a compelling portrait. Photograph by P.L. Hartley

The only difference between these two pictures is that the one on the right was taken using a green filter to strengthen the tone of the lips.

pay attention to a few points. Remember that how they sit will affect how the picture looks. Watch out for the gradual slump that occurs when people sit down for a while, and counter it by asking your subject to sit up and lift their neck and head. At first, this will be too exaggerated for a picture, but as they relax the pose will look natural and alert.

It is a very bad idea to start off with the chair facing directly towards the camera both because it produces boring poses and because it can intimidate your sitter. A better starting point is to have the chair facing almost at right-angles to the camera, then to have your subject lean onto the arm nearest the camera. By placing the entire forearm on the arm of the chair, and bringing the other hand over to grasp the wrist, the shoulders are naturally turned towards the camera. Moving the forearm further back along the chair arm helps to increase the angle of turn. Having used this technique to give an idea of the pose, you should then ask your sitter to stand up and sit down again in the same pose. This will help to avoid the rigid look that people sometimes get when they are posed in an unnatural way.

Another technique is to place the chair facing exactly away from the camera, then ask your subject to sit on the chair leaning on the back. This only works if the chair has no arms, and a reasonably rigid back, but is a very comfortable way to get your subject looking directly towards the camera. Make sure it suits your subject though. Elderly or less mobile people may find it awkward. Hands can be included in the picture if they add something – perhaps because they are well weathered, or very smooth skinned – but beware of using them otherwise. Be especially wary of hands that seem to appear from the corner of the picture, and may even look like they don't belong to the sitter at all. Note also the comments made in chapter 3 about how hands can be used to suggest mood.

PROPS

Props are a very good way of saying something about the person being photographed. Some props have become rather overworked, in particular pipes and spectacles, but other more imaginative ideas can be very effective. The leaning on the back of a chair pose is a good one for allowing the almost incidental inclusion of a hand-held prop. This could be a book, for example, although books are not far behind in the cliche stakes. Anything that is small enough to be held, without being too distracting, will do. There is also a psychological value to props in that they give the sitter something to hold, both for comfort and for diverting attention from the photographic process.

Make-up does not need to be confined to women for photographs. This picture shows an avid Rocky Horror Show fan, who dressed up to attend the performance.

MAKE-UP

Make-up for the camera is very different from make-up worn in every day life. Even so, many men are unwilling to wear it, except when appearing on television. Fortunately, people expect men to look rough, so make-up is less appropriate than for women. As far as most portrait photography is concerned, make-up will only be available when subjects can do it for themselves, and this will tend to mean women. But it is important that the make-up is suited to the picture, rather than to the sex of the person being photographed. It will not be right for all women, and can look wonderful on men.

Black and white pictures need make-up which is distinctly over the top compared to normal wear. Mascara and eye liner both add enormously to the impact of hard black and white pictures. Portrait photography is very often about eye contact, so it is hardly surprising that eye make-up is so important. Lipstick needs to be stronger than usual, because black and white film tends not to pick up the reds very well. Sometimes it is possible to darken the lips using filters if there is no other alternative, but bear in mind that this will also change all other colour tones, including the skin. A green filter darkens red lipstick. Blusher can also be used to good effect, and as with lipstick it is better to go slightly overboard in order to get a reasonable effect.

Colour portraits are easier, because make-up appears very much as it does in real life. So soft make-up should be used for natural pictures, and harsher make-up for more dramatic results. It is particularly effective if colours in the make-up can be echoed elsewhere in the picture, usually in the colours of clothes. Remember also that hair is a part of make-up, and your subject should have clean and tidy hair if that is what the picture calls for.

ATTENTION TO DETAIL

Good character studies are all about getting everything right, both generally and in detail. This means planning things in advance, and advising your subject of the appropriate clothes, props and make-up. Throughout the shoot you need to watch all these elements, as well as attending to photographic matters. In particular, watch out for hair and jewellery becoming displaced, clothes getting rumpled and make-up shiny.

One final trick is to shoot a few pictures even when your subject is not actually posing.

This shot was originally visualised as doing the crossword in a newspaper. However, a particularly nice expression was caught during the setting up shots. The later poses turned out to be less natural.

Perhaps you could give them something to read, then just take a few shots like this, telling them that you are not actually doing pictures, but are just checking that everything works O.K. The reason for this is not to be devious, but to guard against the possibility that they may not respond well to closely controlled character studies – which allow much less freedom for the sitter than in all other types of portraiture. It also gives your sitter a chance to relax and get used to being in front of the camera.

Whatever else you do, remember that the better you know what kind of picture you want, the more your sitter can be prepared. And it is preparation, both of the photographer and the sitter, that turns a good idea into a good photograph.

6: CHILDREN

INTRODUCTION

From the moment they are born, children are fascinating. Their wonder at the world and the different moods they go through in learning to deal with it, make them excellent photographic subjects. They are spontaneous, innocent and guileless. They can also be awkward, uncooperative and frustrating. Just as you have set up your shot and got a charming pose, your model wanders off or notices what you are up to and puts on an idiotic grin. But stick with it and you will be rewarded with some of your best portraits.

SIZE AND SCALE

Children are small. This may seem obvious, but it is an important factor when you come to photograph them. New babies, up to four weeks old, are so small they may not even fill the viewfinder. You need to think carefully about what lens and camera angle you choose. If you use a close-focusing lens to fill the frame with a small child, you will get an exaggerated perspective. Even a standard lens will distort features, if you get too close. The closest safe distance is about 1.5 metres – which is much more than the minimum focusing range for standard lenses. The only way to get a tight portrait of a baby may be to take a picture from further away, then trim down the print or mask it using a matte overlay (see chapter 12).

Not only are children smaller than adults, their bodies are also differently proportioned, with heads and feet larger in relation to their bodies. A normal or wide-angle lens or a high camera angle exaggerates this, which will probably not be what you want. And yet, this is a very common angle from which children are photographed, because the littleness of children is one of their charms.

Try taking pictures that emphasises a child's size, particularly babies and toddlers, without making them appear distorted. One way to do this is to set the child in an adult world. A toddler could be sat in a large armchair, or dressed up in their parents clothes. Or you could pick out a child's arm or leg and put it next to a grown-up version. A small baby holding its parent's hand is a vivid demonstration of the difference in size. But be careful not to let the adult dominate the picture.

The child's tiny size is emphasised by his position in the corner of the doorway. His bright clothing and tricycle stand out against the dark interior.

GENERAL TECHNIQUES FOR PHOTOGRAPHING CHILDREN

Candid and semi-posed pictures of children are nearly always more successful than formal portraits, as it is their naturalness that makes them such appealing subjects. All their moods are interesting. As well as the smiles, you can get wonderful pictures of children in a rage, in tears, tired, asleep and so on. One of the most fascinating aspects of children is their intense absorption in something that interests them.

But their moods never last long, so you need to be quick if you are to catch them. Make sure a camera is always kept to hand – on a mantlepiece or shelf for easy access. If you have to hunt around for it, you will miss a lot of spontaneous pictures. Preset the camera for typical conditions, and make sure it has plenty of life in its batteries.

Pictures showing children in their environment are very effective, whether the child is at work or play. Children take part in all sorts of photogenic activities. Parks, gardens, circuses, anywhere where children gather, offer loads of photographic opportunities. A telephoto lens, such as a 135mm, or a similar zoom lens, will help to distance you from your subjects, so you can be unobtrusive. Conversely, if you are working in cramped indoor situations you will probably find it better to use a wide-angle lens – but remember the comments in chapter 4 about not trying to cram too much into the picture.

When children are at play, try to use a fast shutter speed (1/250 or faster) in order to freeze their movement. If you can, use a well-lit area and a small aperture. This gives you a wider depth of field, making focusing less critical. Autofocus cameras are also good for snapping action.

Because children are invariably surrounded by clutter, you need to be careful about backgrounds. It is easy to get a plain background for babies, as they are small and relatively static. You can place them on a bed and hang a cloth nearby as a background. Make the most of a baby's rounded contours and the texture of baby clothes and blankets. People often knit and crochet beautiful shawls for babies, which you can use to enhance your pictures.

For larger children, be aware of what's in the background. Try to clear mess if you can do it subtly. Or make it a feature of the picture. A telephoto lens helps here too, as the narrower depth of field means you can put the background out of focus, but you will need

Two pictures showing children's quieter moods.

to focus on your subject more accurately to do this.

You can also experiment with camera angles. If you get really low and look up at a child, you can often put its head against the sky. You can set a child against a lawn or carpet by using a higher camera angle. But try not to exaggerate camera angles too much. In general, you get a more pleasing picture by getting down to the child's level.

The main thing to remember when photographing children is to keep looking at what they are doing all the time, rather than deciding on a particular idea in advance. Watch what

they do and you'll be overwhelmed with potential pictures, but try to impose your preconceptions and you'll probably get nothing at all.

LIGHTING

The best lighting source for photographing children is natural daylight. It is simple and will not distract your models. Children's skin is smooth and delicate, so a hazy day with few shadows is ideal. Bright sunlight brings with it problems of squinting eyes, and features lost in shadow. Whereas this can sometimes be effective for adults, it is rarely the case for children. So if there is bright sunlight, try to take advantage of open shade, and avoid the complexities of fill-in flash which is poorly suited to restless children.

If you can use natural light indoors, do so. It is likely that you will need a fast film, and will have to keep quite close to areas lit by window light, but the results will be far more natural than when using flash. Small rooms painted in light colours will reflect light much better than large dark ones, and so are much more suitable. Conveniently, nurseries are often bright, and make excellent settings for portraits of babies. If the light from the window is too harsh, you can diffuse it with a net curtain. Failing this, you may be able to take photographs at a different time of day, when light doesn't come directly through the window, or else find another window which has softer light (north-facing windows are best).

If you have to use flash, avoid aiming it directly at children because the harsh results are highly inappropriate. It is better to bounce the flash off the walls or ceiling, although this risks picking up the colour of the decor. You should also be aware that most flashguns emit a high pitched whine that could disturb young children.

Another complication particularly with young children is that they have very delicate skin tones. It is quite

possible that a brightly coloured object would put a cast on the skin, and look rather peculiar in the finished photograph. Even green grass can do this if there is strong light, in much the same way that gold reflectors can be used to give tans to pale skinned models. The grass problem doesn't usually apply with adults, but is a very real danger for shorter children.

BUILDING UP A RELATIONSHIP

This is probably the most important aspect of photographing children. Children are horribly honest, so if they don't like and trust you, you've had it. Be prepared to give up gracefully if your model is not willing to co-operate. On the other hand, most children are inclined to be friendly, and like having their picture taken. The exception is at about two or three, when a lot of toddlers go through a shy phase, although this is not a problem if you want to take your own children – and have plenty of patience! Another problem age occurs in early teens, when children start to assert their independence. The real art of child portraiture, as with any other kind, is knowing when to press the shutter – and when not to. Be patient and use lots

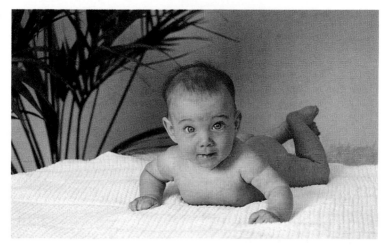

Young babies are relatively immobile, so they can easily be placed on a blanket to be photographed.

of film, nobody except you need see the shots that didn't work.

Photographing other people's children

Photographing other people's children can be fraught with difficulties. If you see a particularly appealing child in a park or playground, get to know the parents first. Never approach a young child directly. Children are warned not to speak to strangers, and these days, an innocent request could seem to have sinister overtones. However, most parents are delighted to have a photographer show interest in their offspring. Also, children respond better to people they know. Parents make extremely useful assistants, distractions, comforters and props. You can get a lovely shot of a baby securely held over a parent's shoulder, or of a child playing in the sandpit with a protective adult looking on from the background.

Photographing babies and young children

Babies are happiest when they've just been fed or at bathtime. A white, enamel bath is especially good, as you will get strong reflected light with a minimum of shadows. However, high technology cameras do not take well to water. A water-resistant compact camera would be

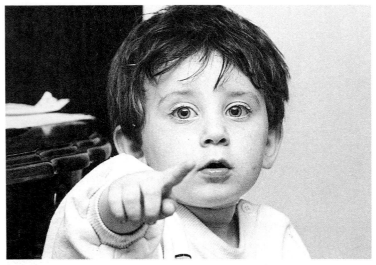

The photographer took advantage of the child's interest in the camera to capture a lively expression of curiosity. Lighting was by flash bounced off a low ceiling.

safer, and doubles up for the beach or under a hosepipe shower in the back garden.

Baby's first steps can give you some really cute pictures. Rather than manoeuvring the baby so that it walks towards the camera, it is better to watch where the baby is heading, then focus on that spot and wait. If necessary, you should move yourself, but beware of following a toddler around or you will make it uneasy. Once children learn to move, they really move. This is great for action pictures, but it makes life very difficult if you want a portrait.

Watch out too for other firsts; the first smile, the first day at school, and the first party. School events can yield lots of possibilities, such as playing musical instruments or organised games and sports days. But take care when you go to a school play. Small children tend to look lost on a large stage and if you try to get closer, you risk embarrassing your children. They may never forgive you for that. Young children and the family pet are another good combination.

Your dignity is of no value to you as far as photographing young children is concerned, and you should be prepared to get down on your hands and knees to play if necessary. Primary school children in particular love to play the fool, so you might as well make that work for, rather than against, you. You can also set children a task to distract them from the camera. No matter what you do, don't forget that young children lose interest very quickly so use the KISS rule – Keep It Short and Simple.

Controlled pictures, like portraits, are best done at times when active toddlers are naturally confined. A high chair can be invaluable here.

Never expect children to keep still while you get your gear ready. Even if they don't move, they'll sulk.

Older children

As children get older they sometimes come to regard photography as an intrusion and it is important that you realize this. The success of your picture sessions is likely to depend much more on how your subject feels. There is also a certain novelty to being photographed by somebody new, so it may well be easier to photograph somebody else's children than your own.

Some of the most successful pictures of children are taken when they are unaware of the camera. In this case, the children were competing in a junior ballroom dancing championship. Off-centre composition has added to the atmosphere of the event.

The photograph was taken using soft, natural, window light and from outside.

head positions. If you want half- or full-length portraits, look out for similarities in dress, or perhaps seat children in similar chairs. Don't forget to watch for similar expressions – perhaps the most interesting type of family resemblance.

Parents and children

One group you're very likely to want to photograph is parents with their children. You won't have any trouble getting loving expressions on the parents' faces, but what you're probably after is the moment of contact between parent and child. Children respond easily to their parents, so try to get the parent to direct the child from within the picture. This could take the form of the parent pointing things out, including the camera. You could also try singing songs, but be careful of getting open mouths in the picture. Small children love playing physical games with their parents, such as being held up high or being given a piggy back or shoulder ride. You could even get an unusual picture of a child held upside down. Watch out for the different shapes parents and children can make together, for example, when playing on a see-saw.

Picturing parents and children in their environment can also be very effective. Children often play at the tasks their parents are doing. One example of this might be making a miniature pie whilst Mum or Dad cooks the dinner. Parents teaching their children new skills also make good subjects for joint portraits.

Here are two different approaches to teenage portraits; one is more moody and stylish, while the other is closer to a studio style pose.

7: PEOPLE IN CONTEXT

INTRODUCTION

Adding context to a portrait means broadening the scope of the picture to include a sense of its setting. In this chapter, we will be looking at two kinds of photographs showing people in context. Location portraits are a record of where a person was, using the setting as a backdrop, rather than saying anything about the person themselves. Many holiday photographs fall into this category. Often you won't have much control over the situation, and it will be important to work quickly to avoid boring your subjects.

Environmental portraits are rather more individual and are used to give additional information about the person being photographed. The surroundings will usually be somewhere the person works or lives – a craftsman in his workshop, for example. Usually you have much more control in environmental portraits, and can rearrange the background or even use your own lighting equipment. Since the person being photographed could be engaged in an activity, it is much less important to have eye contact with the camera. This means environmental portraits can look almost candid, whereas in fact they are usually very carefully set up.

We will be concentrating on location photographs taken outside and environmental photographs taken inside, as this is often another way of distinguishing between the two.

WHERE PEOPLE ARE

For a location portrait to succeed, the place where it was taken must be identifiable. Sometimes the identification can be generic – such as a landscape or seaside background. On other occasions the location will be unique, maybe a well-known landmark or even a place name will be included in the picture. The important thing is that the location is an intrinsic part of the final photograph. It may be that the person in the photograph is less identifiable, perhaps they have their back to the camera and are looking out over the scene. This doesn't necessarily stop the photograph being a portrait, but you should beware of overdoing this rather more subtle approach.

Using the location
Always start with the location itself. Before you put your camera to your eye, get a feel for the location. Are you actually in the right place for the photograph? Be aware of objects you don't want in your picture, such as washing lines

and telephone wires. Where will you pose your sitter? Can you use the person to hide parts of the location you don't want in the picture? Would you get a better picture by stepping back, or moving to the side? What about kneeling down, or standing on something to get higher up? All this should be considered before you look through your camera. The idea is to eliminate distracting elements within the picture, and to make a good composition. You need not even have the person physically in place at this stage – what matters is to compose the photograph in the most effective way. The composition should be used to unite the person and the place, such that one would be incomplete without the other. This is really a process of visualising how you want the finished picture to look, and you should allow yourself plenty of freedom to imagine the result however you like. It is unwise to start off looking through the camera, because this restricts your view and so limits your imagination. Bold visualisation can lead to really dramatic results.

The next step is to see how closely you can approach your visualised idea with the equipment available and within the physical limitations that apply. The direction and

A holiday photograph taken outside the Dome of the Rock in Jerusalem. It works well because both the location and the person can be clearly seen. Coincidentally, a great feeling of harmony is achieved by the variety of blue tones.

intensity of natural lighting may well impose restrictions on the angle you choose, particularly with regard to how shadows and harsh light affect your sitter.

Depth of field
Location portraits are usually taken with wide angle or standard lenses, because they

83

Rather than closing in on the shooter and his gun, the composition here allows plenty of space to reflect the expanse of the countryside.

can include large areas and offer considerable depth of field, even at modest aperture settings. Many compact cameras have lenses which fall into this category.

Focusing is critical. It is important that the person in the picture is completely sharp, and that the background is also sharp enough to be recognised. If either of these elements is not sharp, then the picture is liable to fail as a location portrait. Autofocus cameras can present a problem, as they usually focus on whatever is in the centre of the frame. This is unlikely to be your subject. A focus lock is

particularly important here, so you can focus on the model, then recompose the picture.

Any lens of standard focal length or shorter is likely to give a recognisable background, regardless of how the aperture is set. To be more exact, the precise aperture required to have the background and foreground both properly sharp can be found by focusing on the two areas separately and then setting the aperture needed for sufficient depth of field. Suppose, for example, that you are using a standard 50mm lens on a 35mm camera. The background is so far away that

A 28mm wide angle lens stopped down to give generous depth of field has given a high degree of sharpness to all elements of the picture.

when the lens is focused it is set to infinity (∞), and the person in the foreground is 5 metres from the camera. You can the reset the lens so that the ∞ marker and the 5m marker are equally spaced on opposite sides of the lens focussing mark. By looking to see which aperture setting takes in both markers, you can determine what f-stop is required to have the whole photograph sharp. In the case of the 50mm lens, the f-stop required is f/11, but if a 28mm lens were used under the same conditions, an aperture of f/4 would be sufficient. Conversely, there isn't a

135mm lens made which has a small enough aperture to keep everything sharp in this example – a good proof that longer focal length lenses are less suitable on location.

Posing on location

Having visualised and framed the scene, and also chosen an appropriate lens and aperture for the required angle of view and depth of field, the final element is to pose your subject. In general, off-centre posing is best as it allows plenty of space to show the location itself. Very often, location portraits are ideal candidates for posing according to the rule of thirds. If you place your subject right in the middle of the picture, the background will tend to be broken up.

A useful guide when trying to set the balance between the person and the background is to remember that we are used to reading from left to right, and to look at photographs in the same way. This means our attention is drawn to what is on the left of the picture, because that is the area we look at first. You can use this tendency by putting what is most important to your picture, either the person or an area of background, on the left.

Another useful tip is to include something other than just the person in the foreground. Rather than having a torso appearing out of the bottom of the picture, ask your subject to sit down or lean on a convenient prop. It doesn't look natural to have people standing square on to the camera with their arms folded – in fact, people only ever seem to stand like that to have their picture taken. Steps and low walls can be used as convenient benches, and sitting people down has the added advantage of giving them a chance to relax a little. If you want your subject standing, use hands, feet, the angle of the head and so on to make the posing more

imaginative. Try getting your subject to look at a particular point of interest in the background or even out into the distance, if the setting is an open landscape.

WHAT PEOPLE DO

Surroundings form an intrinsic part of environmental portraits, providing additional information about the person photographed. You will usually have the full co-operation of your subject and a large measure of control over the picture. Again, bold visualisation is really worthwhile, giving you a starting point from which to achieve the exact effect you want. Start by asking yourself questions, which become gradually more specific, so that you can move from a general idea to an actual photograph.

If you can, check out the location well beforehand to get an idea of what the light will be like and what equipment you will need. Some questions are best answered before you arrive to take the picture. Should the picture be shot in colour or black and white? Would it help the atmosphere

The camera angle was carefully chosen, here, not only to show the guard and his van, but also to add a feeling of toughness to the picture.

The photographer asked radiator restorer, Harry Packham, to ignore the camera. Careful exposure was needed to keep detail in the shadow areas, without losing the gas flame. Kodak Tri-X was used at ISO 800 and developed for 12 minutes in diluted D-76.

for it to be a bit grainy, or should the tones be as smooth as possible? Is the available light strong enough? And is it the right quality – coming from the best direction and sufficiently diffused, or otherwise, for your needs? What is the range of brightnesses between highlight and shadow and can your film cope with this? Which will be the best lens to take in the angle of coverage you want, and what aperture will be required for the necessary depth of field? Will you need a tripod so that you can use a slow shutter speed, and if so, then is there enough room to set one up?

Equipment for environmental portraits

Keep your equipment as simple as possible to get the picture you want. There are two main reasons for this. First, the less equipment you have to worry about, the more you can concentrate on the picture itself. Second, a lot of elaborate paraphernalia can distract your subject, making it much harder for you to get a natural pose. Remember that when taking an important picture is not the time to be trying out new equipment, and you will have to practise with it in advance.

Flash and available light
A small flashgun to lighten dark shadows could be very useful. Flash should be unobtrusive and used only for fill-in. You could just use a powerful flashgun and set it to a lower power setting. Interiors abound with many flash hazards – especially highly reflective surfaces which cause very unpleasant flare in the picture. Flash lighting can also kill the natural atmosphere that existed in the original scene. In the wrong circumstances, flash could even be dangerous, because the flash trigger circuit could ignite any flammable gas or even disrupt sensitive electronic equipment.

Choosing the best angle
There are two distinct ways of photographing people in their environment. Either the person can be involved in what they are doing, and seemingly unaware of the camera, or they can be looking towards the camera – as if they had taken a momentary break from their activity. The approach required for each type of picture is somewhat different.

Pictures of people concentrating on their activities are better photographed by available light. This gives a more natural feel and is therefore more consistent with the pose. Although the photograph should look natural, and almost candid, there is no reason why it should not be carefully set-up to achieve the effect you want. It is very important, however, that the pose looks convincing. Try asking your subject to carry on with the activity and to ignore your photography. You may find this presents you with natural poses anyway. Otherwise, you can ask your subject to change position slightly, perhaps a hand moved out of the way or the head turned a bit, to give you a clear view. A special advantage of such pictures is that they don't require eye contact between the subject and the camera. This makes them well suited to people who are nervous. Avoiding eye contact also puts more emphasis on what the person is doing. This means that if, for example, you wanted a picture of a blacksmith at work, then you would be better avoiding eye contact. If, on the other hand, you wanted a portrait of the blacksmith himself, you might prefer to have eye contact.

Another consideration is the intimacy of the picture. There

are definite differences between somebody standing outside a workshop, the same person standing within the workshop and the person actually working. The pictures look progressively less posed, and more natural, but in fact they can all be equally controlled – it is just the finished result which looks different.

Finding the right angle

Never be content just to take a photograph from one viewpoint. Move around, see how the framing changes and how the emphasis switches from the person to their activity. Take a good range of photographs, then compare the results to see what worked and what didn't. Sometimes you will be able to make minor adjustments to the picture at the printing stage, especially in the case of darkening distracting objects, but you should always try to be aware of the problems before you take the pictures. While you are moving around, take care of your subject. Try to move slowly and be friendly.

You will often find that there is one particular place for taking pictures which is better than all the others. Look for a position with the light behind you to make sure that you are not photographing into shadow. At the same time, if

your subject is doing something which involves working close to an object, there will often be one angle which shows things more clearly. Right-handed people are best photographed from their left because it avoids having their right arm blocking the camera. Conversely, the same people sometimes tilt their head to look to the right, so a clearer view of their face can sometimes be had from the right-hand side.

When you have the results, don't forget to show them to whoever you photographed. Often people do not have good photographs of themselves in their own surroundings, and they will be very grateful for copies. Most people think of portraits as something done in a formal studio, but many people actually prefer to see themselves engaged in a more natural activity. This is an area where any keen photographer can have the edge over a formal studio. It was one of the fascinations of the early Victorian photographers to be able to record people in their natural surroundings, without the artificiality of a studio. By developing your techniques for environmental portraits you will be carrying on an excellent tradition that is unavailable to most high street studios.

8: CANDID AND ACTION

INTRODUCTION

We have grouped candid and action pictures together because they need a similar approach. In both cases, the act of taking pictures must not disturb the subjects being photographed. This means that you cannot set up shots, but have to react to events as they happen.

BEING UNOBTRUSIVE

Being unobtrusive is as much a state of mind as it is a matter of physical reality. There is a technique of using very long focal length lenses from far away, but it can put you in the position of a Peeping Tom. The essence of candid photography is not to spy on people, but to capture them at their most natural. This means being able to react quickly to catch spontaneous moments. Autofocus cameras with autoexposure and relatively wide-angle lenses are ideal. Another advantage of compact cameras is that they can be carried around all the time,

These two pictures show two very different weddings. The shot of the Christian bride and groom was taken as they were having a rest between the official photographer's poses. It is the pageboy's expression which makes the picture. Hindu weddings are much more relaxed than formal church services. Guests are free to wander around, participate and take photographs.

The photographer took this picture from a balcony as guests assembled for a New Year's Eve party.

and are therefore available to take a picture whenever an opportunity arises.

As soon as you raise a camera to your eye, you warn people that a photograph is about to be taken, so try to learn to use your camera without looking through the viewfinder. You need to predict what the framing will be, and you also have to be aware that autofocus cameras focus on the centre of the picture – whatever it may be. Some compact cameras have a viewfinder on the top plate, so that they can be used at waist height, like the old box cameras. Since people are

unused to this technique nowadays, it is very much easier to use such a camera without attracting attention.

You only have to be unobtrusive before taking the photograph, so there is no reason not to use flash. Nobody can react fast enough, in response to a flash burst, to prevent the picture being taken, so you need only worry about how people will respond afterwards.

RESPECT FOR PRIVACY

One reason why candid photographers like to remain unobtrusive, and sometimes shun the use of flash, is because they are unsure of the reactions that their picture taking will evoke. This raises a serious question about the motives of photographers, and the degree to which they respect the privacy of their subjects.

Moslem women in purdah go to extreme lengths to hide themselves in the interests of modesty, and are greatly offended by being photographed. Many other people also regard the camera with suspicion. Candid photographers should never cause their subjects embarrassment or offence, and would be better advised not take photographs in such situations, rather than having to resort to clandestine behaviour.

CANDID PHOTOGRAPHY

Candid photography is about everyday life and events and the candid photographer should turn his or her attention to ordinary happenings. Children's toys have come and gone, including hoola hoops, Rubik cubes and skateboards, and pictures of children using them are now historical documents as much as they are photographs. At one time it would have been unremarkable to see children playing with a clockwork train, but now it is very rare. Attitudes and political concerns can also be recorded, as can the changing lifestyles of communities. Obviously, it is possible to set up posed pictures to illustrate these things, but nothing is quite as convincing as a good candid shot. Many of the classic photographs by great photojournalistic photographers are simply candid records of what was going on, and yet they have become respected as some of the greatest photographs ever.

Special occasions, such as weddings and parties, yield excellent opportunities for candid photography. The pictures can capture the special magic of an event people will want to look back on over the years. The trick is to reflect the atmosphere of the occasion, using visual clues to show what was going on. There is often a professional photographer at special events, particularly at weddings. When the professional sets up a shot, everyone else crowds round to catch the same picture. These photographs are likely to be disappointing, because nobody else will have the same range of equipment as the official photographer.

So what sort of pictures should you be taking? Official photographers often have a rather rigid set of pictures they have to take. As a guest, you are much freer. Shots of people reacting to what is happening can be particularly evocative. You can also take the opportunity to experiment with films, poses, camera angles and so on. Rather than copying what the professional does, you can complement his or her work. For example, weddings are almost always shot in colour with lots of flash, so why not take your candids on black and white film, and use available light?

Techniques for candid photography

Photographers are sometimes too embarrassed to take out their camera on the spur of the moment. This is a definite hindrance to photography in general, and to candid pictures in particular. One way to solve this problem is to carry a compact camera with you all the time and to set out to shoot a roll of film every week. The intention would simply be to photograph little snippets of life – events that strike you as being amusing or interesting. In fact, anything you might tell somebody about at a later date is probably worth a picture.

You cannot expect every picture to be a winner, but there are steps you can take to help ensure a high degree of success. First, you should make

sure you can use the camera without even having to look at the controls. Know exactly where the backlight compensation button is, and the focus and exposure locks if it has automatic controls. If there is either aperture or shutter priority, make sure that it is kept at a midway setting and that you know what that setting is. Manual focus cameras are best kept set for the hyperfocal distance,· because more is likely to be in focus that way. This is about 10m at f/8 for a 50mm lens. Remember though, that if you change the aperture you will also change the hyperfocal distance. This technique is, therefore, most useful with aperture priority cameras.

With candid photography, it is always better to take one picture immediately, then worry about checking focus, exposure, and framing afterwards. If you do it the other way around the moment may have passed before you are ready.

Another way to practise is to set yourself a project. Street markets and fairs are both good hunting grounds for candid pictures, and both usually give a high proportion of interesting results. You could be even more specific, and aim to record different approaches to a particular side-show at a fair, such as a test of strength. If you are hanging around one event, and taking lots of photographs, people are more likely to accept you. You may have to explain yourself occasionally, but don't be afraid to do so.

A rather offbeat, and very original, candid project was published in a photographic magazine some years ago. A mini-cab driver took pictures of his customers getting in and out of the cab. The results were highly amusing, but since none of the people could be identified there was no danger of causing embarrassment. In many ways it was the epitome of good candid photography.

ACTION PHOTOGRAPHY

When photographing action, and especially sports, it is important not to distract your subject – but what that means can vary widely. Professional golfers sometimes get upset just by hearing a quiet shutter click at the wrong moment, whereas boxers are often unaware of motor drives and powerful flashguns, and buskers positively encourage photography if it improves the tips! Make sure you are not getting in the way of what's going on. In general though, participants have other things to think about without noticing photographers, and you will quickly be told if you are causing a nuisance.

Celebrities often participate in local publicity events, and it is usually easy for members of the public to get a good position from which to take pictures. In this case, Gloria Hunniford was opening a new estate agent's office in Petts Wood, Bromley.

Action photography is usually associated with pictures bursting with drama, although this is not always the case. The equipment you will require depends on the balance of how close you can get physically, and how much closer you need to get optically. There is no doubt that major sporting events are the hardest to photograph, because only a select number of professional photographers

95

Top snooker players frequently play exhibition matches at small local clubs, where amateurs can take pictures away from the limitations of prestige competitions.

are given the freedom to move about to get the best angles. It would be foolish to go to such events expecting to get the kind of pictures which fill the sports pages of newspapers, but you can get very exciting photographs by confining yourself to less prestigious events.

It is not even true that the standard of performance is worse at smaller events, because these are the events which yield the Olympic champions of years to come. But it is true that good

photographs do need good people who are dedicated to their sport, because only when the competitors are putting everything into the event, can the pictures have real impact. It is very common to be able to identify the best athletes as those which give the best pictures, and you would do well to concentrate on them.

Not all action is sport. Jugglers, acrobats and circus acts, for example, all provide action which can yield excellent pictures. Sometimes you will have to take photographs from an allocated seat, but at other times you may find a busking juggler who provides almost limitless opportunities. Remember though, that buskers are trying to earn money when they perform, so be sure to make a contribution if you have been taking pictures–or even if you just enjoyed the show.

Equipment for action photography

Different equipment is best suited to different sports, but there are certain lenses which are most useful. A 70–210mm zoom lens can be used for a lot of sports pictures, although there will be times when you cannot get close enough to get a decent-sized image even when using the longer focal length setting. This is particularly true of some field sports, and of action events where you are confined to your seat.

If you are very serious about sport and action, you may well find a long focal length lens helpful. Although professional photographers often use very bulky lenses, costing several thousand pounds, there are cheaper alternatives which are more than adequate for most events and which are used by some professionals who don't want the bulk or the expense of the larger lenses. The Sigma Apo 400mm F/5.6 is one such

lens, offering good quality at a sensible price. It is also light and compact. But, as we have said before, don't go out and buy a special piece of equipment like this unless you are sure that you will use it regularly.

A popular alternative to buying a long focal length lens is to invest in a teleconverter. The most common type doubles the focal length of any lens with which it is used. This may sound ideal, especially given that converters start at a few tens of pounds, but they have their disadvantages. The worst is that they reduce the lens aperture by as much as they increase the focal length. So a 200mm f/4, becomes a 400mm f/8 when a 2x teleconverter is used. This is a full f-stop slower than the Sigma lens. Converters also magnify defects within the lens to which they are coupled, and need to be matched to particular lenses for best results.

Like working in a home studio, the important thing is that you work within the limitations of the equipment you have and that the event imposes. If you don't have a long focal length lens, then adjust your picture taking to what equipment you do have. Some sports are particularly good for getting in close, so that even a standard, or wide-angle, lens can be used to good effect.

FILM FOR SPORTS PHOTOGRAPHY

Sports photography often calls for films in the extreme. If colour is important, it needs to be captured on brilliant colour film (usually transparency), but if colour adds nothing then it is better to work in black and white. Often a grainy film gives a gritty picture appropriate to the raw effort of most sports. This is less true of the graceful sports, such as women's gymnastics, but it is a good general rule.

Note that there has been no mention, so far, of using fast film to allow fast shutter speeds to freeze the action. Of course, shutter speeds have to be considered, but they are not the whole story. You should regard choosing film as an artistic decision, not one based solely on the technical requirements of the situation. It could well be that a given lighting condition would allow exposures of 1/250 second at f/8, or 1/1000 second at f/4 – and there would be good reasons for choosing either alternative. The first would give good depth of field with normal lenses (or maybe the minimum aperture when using a teleconverter), whereas the latter would be better for freezing movement, and would also help the sharply focused subject stand out from the background. What you shouldn't be doing, is choosing a high speed film just to enable you to use 1/1000 second at f/8, because you can't decide whether the shutter speed or aperture setting is more important.

For the times when you do have to use a high speed film, it is important to know how you can make the grain look less obvious. Grain is most apparent in smooth mid-tones, especially those which are not particularly colourful, so try to avoid these situations when using colour film. If you find yourself up against this problem, it is likely that you should be shooting in black and white. Another tactic concerns the size of photographed details compared to the grain size. Whilst it may be acceptable to do a tightly composed shot on grainy film, a wider view, where everything appears that much smaller, is unlikely to be acceptable.

GENERAL TECHNIQUES FOR SPORTS PHOTOGRAPHY

Sport is about people – and it is

This stunt rider was captured at the peak of a wheelie. Mixed flash and blur adds to the effect of action.

These two pictures illustrate opposite approaches to sport. In one case, a wide angle lens has been used for dramatic perspective and good depth of field, whilst in the other, a telephoto lens has been used at full aperture to isolate the netball player.

important that your pictures show this. Whether you go for a reflective shot of a boxer in his corner, or a gymnast poised ready to leap, or whether you prefer the excitement of the winning line, or a tumbler performing cartwheels, all the pictures would be stronger for showing the people's faces clearly.

Sports can either be regarded as consisting of a series of exciting moments, or for the general atmosphere of the event. The latter is a much safer type of shot, because timing is not so critical, and there is an opportunity to check the framing and focusing before taking the picture. If successful, the first type of photograph is very much more dramatic, and is often an award winner, but it is a matter of luck as well as constant practice to get it right.

Capturing peak excitement
All action has a peak moment, but this is more predictable in some cases than in others. Sports, for example, can be graded by how easy this is to do. Long jumping is very easy to photograph, because the peak moment occurs on landing, and all competitors land in very much the same place. Goal scoring sports are slightly more difficult because although you know where the excitement will occur, you

don't know when, or from what angle or distance the attack will come. Team sports tend to give you clues, because there are often set pieces, or favoured players you can watch out for. Individual combat sports, on the other hand, are really difficult because they are so fast, and if they were predictable, opponents would be able to avoid being defeated. Non-competitive events are generally the easiest to predict, since they usually run to a routine, and peak moments are built up to at intervals.

Getting sharp pictures
Having identified some action to photograph, both in terms of having the right equipment and opportunities, you need to consider the practicalities of getting sharp pictures. This means pictures which are both accurately focused, and also where the action has been frozen. This is the familiar balance of shutter speeds and lens apertures. But when you are practising to improve your action photography, it is important that you only work on one thing at a time. If you cannot focus your lens, it doesn't matter how fast a shutter speed you use. Autofocus lenses may be helpful, provided the main subject is in the centre of the viewfinder, but you can be

sure that there won't be enough time to use the focus lock before the action has moved on.

There are two ways to improve your manual focusing, depending on whether you are prepared to risk getting nothing sharp at all! The most critical method means working with the lens set at its widest aperture all the time, thus making focusing so critical that only when the lens is precisely focused will the subject be sharp. The other technique is to use smaller apertures whilst practising, then to move to wider apertures as your focusing gets more proficient. This tends to produce more pictures which are of average quality, but is unlikely to produce any real stunners until you progress to the wider apertures.

Focusing is easy to assess in finished prints, because something in the picture should always be sharp, and it is just a matter of making sure that the something coincides with the centre of interest. Movement is rather more difficult to check, since it can be due either to camera movement or to subject movement. The two can be distinguished depending on whether or not the background is blurred, as it will be if the camera moved. A complicating factor here is that

the background is normally well out of focus, and this makes it harder to decide if it is blurred.

Camera movement can be reduced by using a support, and monopods are particularly convenient for action work. Subject movement can be reduced either by increasing the shutter speed within the limitations of the available apertures and the accuracy of your focusing, or by changing your angle of view. Motion across the viewfinder is more likely to blur than that coming directly towards, or going away from, the camera. So if you are using a slowish shutter speed which means anything slower than about 1/500 second, and you want to freeze action, you should choose a head-on angle if possible.

Atmospheric action pictures
Sometimes you may not want to show peak action at all, but would rather capture the atmosphere of the event. Photographs showing masses of runners at the start of marathons fall into this category, because they are showing the scale of the event rather than the running itself. Similarly, a scenic country village cricket green may lend itself to a beautiful landscape, in which the game is almost incidental, but an important part of the picture

Minority sports can yield excellent results. The photographer's imagination and creativity matter more than the sport's popularity. This picture was taken at a leisure centre during an open day when it was easy to get close to the activities. A 28mm lens was used, with flash to freeze the action pin-sharp.

nevertheless. Or even a trapeze artist set within the context of the complete big top.

Composition and creativity are much more important in atmospheric pictures, than in action photographs. This means that you should hunt around for the best angle, and make sure that the background is appropriate to the feel of the picture. When using colour film, you need to be wary of the background, where a small splash of colour can distract from the main subject, and ruin the picture completely. In black and white, the tones and shapes become more important. This can be used to effect by creating silhouettes – if the lighting is suitable.

9: STYLE

INTRODUCTION

Photographic style is what makes the pictures you take yours and nobody else's. It is where photography becomes art. No two photographers will take the same picture of the same event or person, because no two people see things in the same way. But style cannot take the place of technique. You need a good solid technique from which to develop your style.

AN EXAMPLE OF STYLE

Throughout this chapter we have used pictures of a single person, taken by a number of different photographers. The idea of the project was to illustrate what style means in practical terms. Some of the photographers are professional and some are amateur. The results cannot show how the different photographers approached their subject, but where possible we have given information in the captions. This includes how long the pictures took to take, what equipment was used, and what the original intention was.

STYLE VERSUS CONTENT

One of the problems of style is that it can overpower the picture. A good photograph needs to balance content against style, so that both contribute to the end product, rather than competing with each other. This is where the cultivation of style can be counterproductive. Fashion magazines sometimes include photographs which are so abstract that it is hard to decide what they are trying to depict. This may be acceptable for fashion, but it is not so suitable for portraits. Creating bizarre images for the sake of being different is a shallow way to look at style.

ELEMENTS OF STYLE

It is very difficult to say what constitutes style, which is why it is developed, rather than learnt. Style should be a natural response to what you are photographing. Perhaps the first thing you need to do is to examine your own responses to the world and work out what you are trying to express through your photography.

This picture was shot in Golders Green Park in the early afternoon of a bright sunny day, using red and polarising filters to darken the sky. A Tokina 28–70mm F/3.5 lens was used to give the dramatic perspective. Photographed by keen amateur, Trevor Spiro, using Ilford HP5 Plus film and printed on Ilford Multigrade.

This does not have to be violent emotions against a background of social history although it could be. You might simply want to put your own quirky sense of humour into your pictures.

That said, there are some obvious devices that can be used to bring an element of stylistic consistency to your photography, and provide a step towards developing your own personal style. What you

Paul Barsby is a professional wedding and portrait photographer, who runs Shutterbug Photography in Bromley. He used Fuji Reala film for particularly natural skin tones. The whole session took about 20 minutes and used two rolls of 120 roll film (total of 24 photographs).

need to do is to isolate elements of your work that you like and think are effective and see how you can use these elements in other pictures.

Going to extremes

The concept of compromise is perhaps the most destructive factor in developing style. You should decide what you want to achieve and go all out for it. If you marvel at professional photographs of beautiful landscapes, with perfect detail and not a hint of grain, then you will have to use the best film available, and a sturdy tripod. A large format camera would help, but you will go a long way with 35mm if you use it well. Similarly, if you want to get really gritty social documentary pictures, then use a grainy black and white film.

If you need maximum depth of field, then use the smallest aperture you've got in conjunction with a good tripod, rather than a high speed film with fast shutter speeds and a hand-held camera. For sharp action, use the fastest shutter speed, practise your focusing, and only use fast film if the subject warrants it.

Whatever your preference, try going to extremes and see what you come up with. Don't despair if your first results aren't perfect. Experiment and allow yourself to fail, work out

what went wrong, then have another go.

Mood

Rather than photographing subjects as they stand, try to evoke a mood which says something about your attitude to your subject, or your subjects' attitude to their environment. If you decided to photograph commuters for example, would you want them to look happy or sad, grey or colourful, organised or following like sheep? Don't fall into the trap of showing people in a stereotyped way if you don't happen to believe it. In particular, it has always been fashionable for black and white photography to be rather gloomy, yet Robert Doisneau's joyful scenes of French life are popular as black and white posters. If you fail to think about your own feelings, and just follow convention, you will never cultivate your own style.

Lighting

One of the most useful features of a studio is in allowing you to control the light. As we said in chapter 2, lighting isn't just a matter of how much light, but of what quality. Not only is it used to illuminate the subject, it also sets the mood – and therefore the style of the picture.

The kind of lights you use are important, whether they

Rachel Braverman used Kodak P3200 high speed film so that this shot could be taken entirely by available light to capture the atmosphere of a sports changing room. The inspiration for the photograph came from having seen the potential when changing after a squash match.

are flash or tungsten, and whether they are aimed directly at the model or bounced off large reflectors. On a more subtle level, you can decide on whether catchlights should be seen in the sitter's eyes, and what size or number there should be. In extreme cases, people wearing sunglasses could be arranged so that a large white panel reflects in the whole of one lens, whilst the other is completely black, for example.

Having set up the lighting, and metered the correct exposure, you can decide if it would be more appropriate not to use the meter's recommended settings. Both over- and under-exposure can be effective. The point of technique here is knowing what effect the different exposures will have. It is not a question of modifying the exposure to suit the subject, over-exposing for women and under-exposing for men, but rather to achieve a particular feel in your pictures. If you prefer to photograph people in a serious mood, then it may be better to have them looking directly towards the camera with sombre lighting, and to avoid light coloured clothing.

Backgrounds
The background is an important part of the picture. It should complement the subject, and how you use it could also be part of your identity as a photographer. Painted studio backdrops are effective, but expensive. Outdoor locations are more readily available, and can be more inspiring. Angular architecture and country fields are two extremes, but there are many other alternatives. By adopting a low angle, you could frame all your portraits against the sky, making use of dramatic clouds or colours. Using a flashgun to light the foreground enables you to make the background darker, a technique much used by portrait photographer Terry O'Neill. Shooting on black and white film makes it easy to superimpose cloud formations in the darkroom.

Cathy Corr wanted to achieve a very stylish effect. She brought along jackets and hats to the studio session and used very dramatic tungsten lighting. She has just started out as a freelance photographer after working in the music industry for several years.

Equipment
Photographs are composed in the camera, so the type of equipment you use is bound to affect your style. The format you use affects the kind of pictures you take, whether you use elongated 35mm or square 6×6. This is a far more important consideration than whether different formats give

109

better quality, and is coupled to the way in which the cameras are used. 35mm cameras are usually held at eye level, whereas larger medium format cameras are often used from the chest or waist. This immediately affects the way you look at people and your relationship with your subjects.

Manipulating photographs

You may get an idea for a picture that is not naturalistic. That is, you can see it in your mind's eye, but it will take some manipulation before you can see it on paper or on slide. There are a large number of techniques you can use to get a distinctive result. Toning is an obvious possibility, and can either be applied to the whole picture or just to a small part of it. Black and white prints can be coloured with water inks, or dyes, to give either an old-fashioned pastel hand coloured result, or a vivid contemporary picture.

Jon Tarrant's photograph was visualised in detail well in advance, so that the make-up artist, Mandy Tenalver, could produce exactly the right effect. The lipstick kiss was hand coloured using Photocolor dyes, and the finished print was rephotographed to make the colouring blend into the picture.

Naina Khambhaita, a scientific and technical photographer, wanted to produce a pastel studio portrait. Soft lighting and high speed film (Konica SR-G 3200 colour negative) combined to give the desired effect.

If you shoot on colour print film, you could get both black and white and colour prints made, then mount them together to present an artistic contrast. Colour slides can be projected onto textured screens, then re-photographed to give a period feel for suitable subjects. They can also be copied and combined with other images. If you have access to a slide copier with a Polaroid holder, you can take instant pictures from your transparencies.

111

Amateur photographers, Ian Banister and Jon Gadd teamed up to explore the different location possibilities of Richmond Park. Ian Banister, whose picture is shown top, used his camera upside down so that a hot shoe mounted flashgun gave a low angle fill-in light.

By using black and white slide film (Agfa Dia-direct, or Kodak T-MAX developed in T-MAX reversal solutions), you can do multiple copies onto colour film using different colour filters. The slides can also be printed directly onto reversal colour paper, for black and white prints with a totally different tonal rendition.

In fact there is no limit to the ways in which seemingly finished pictures can be modified. But remember that manipulations should always be appropriate to the subject photographed, and it is better to know what the final result will be before the picture is taken. That way, you can make any adjustments necessary before pressing the shutter release button.

LOOKING AT STYLE

All the famous name photographers have their own style which has helped to make their work so well-known. So when you are thinking about your own style, look at pictures created by photographers you admire. Examine the subject, location, style of lighting, angle of view, and check for manipulation techniques.

Visit exhibitions by established photographers, and decide why their pictures work so well – or what makes some weaker than others. Popular magazines also use well-known photographers, so start to look for credits on pictures that interest you, and see if the same names keep cropping up. You are very likely to find that, after a little while, you can spot the work of a particular photographer without even checking the picture credit. When this happens, ask yourself what it is that has helped you to identify their work. The answer will probably be the same thing that defines their style.

It may be that, over the years, photographers turn their attention to different subjects. Don McCullin has gone from war to landscapes and on to adverts for the police force. Despite the variety of content, all his pictures have a consistency which makes them uniquely McCullin's. His pictures say something about his approach to photography and to life in general. This is the mark of a true photographer. It is the emotional foundation on which style is based, and without which photographs are simply sterile statements of what happened to be in front of the camera when the shutter was fired. The first step towards developing your style is to realise how you feel about your subjects, and to make sure you communicate that feeling to other people.

10: SOMETHING DIFFERENT

INTRODUCTION

Photography can be thought of as either a technical activity, or an artistic one. If it is technical, then photographs can be judged in terms of how sharp they are, how accurately they record colours, and how well they represent reality in general. If you obey a series of rules you can take a photograph that is technically perfect.

But if you want to consider photography as an art form, then technique is just the beginning. A good understanding of the techniques of photography, what the rules are, why they exist and how they work, is your starting point. In the previous chapter, we talked about what makes your photographs yours. In this chapter, we are going to look at a few ways in which you can go against established techniques when what you want is out of the ordinary.

BREAKING RULES

Once you know how to use a rule, you can go on to break it. The table at the end of this chapter gives a selection of common guidelines for good, conventional, photography and suggestions of the ways in which they can be broken effectively. The alternatives are not designed to give you another set of rules. They are simply ideas to get your imagination going.

HOW TO ACHIEVE THE EFFECTS

We could go on listing examples of alternative ideas, then leave you to experiment in order to find out how they work. But this trial and error approach can be very discouraging at first, so in the following section we have given more details about how the effects can be achieved. One of the most important things about breaking rules is that you must do it boldly. If you are half-hearted about it, your pictures may look as if you made a mistake taking a conventional photograph.

Composition
There is no limit to what you can do in terms of composition. But whatever you do, it must suit both the subject and mood of the photograph. The rule of thirds is most frequently applied to horizontally viewed pictures, so the first thing you could do is to make use of it in uprights. This is harder, because the frame is less wide, giving less separation between the thirds.

Another compositional rule to break is that people should always face into the picture,

This picture was initially shot using orange filtered flash to keep the skin tones accurate whilst allowing daylight to give a blue background on tungsten film. Choice of location, make-up and subsequent copying into Polachrome HC instant slide film have all contributed to the finished effect. Model; Yvonne Covus. Make-up; Melissa Lackersteen. Photograph by Jon Tarrant.

rather than out of it. In fact a good way to give a feeling of alienation or loneliness is to put a person right on the edge of the photograph looking outwards – perhaps using a bleak space in the rest of the picture.

Cropping people

The normal approach to photographing people is to consider how much of them to include in the picture in terms of the length of their body. Head and shoulders, half-length, and full-length all being standard ways of

cropping. As an alternative, why not go for a left or right side, having the other half of the body hidden by an object in the picture, or even out of the picture completely.

People who work with their hands can often be portrayed in this way. A very effective picture of Mohammed Ali, taken by award winning sports photographer, Eamonn McCabe, was simply a life size print of his fist. The temptation to compare it against your own fist, and wonder at the size of Ali's, was overwhelming.

People in uniform, especially

military uniform, can be identified simply by their tunic, which can give a colourful, almost abstract, picture. Even shoes can say a lot about people. A ballet dancer photographed on points, or high heeled fashion shoes worn against black stockinged legs, can both be atmospheric portraits of the people without ever showing their faces.

Distorting colours

Film manufacturers go out of their way to produce films which give accurate colours, but there is always a need to use colour films appropriate to the prevailing light. Most films are balanced for daylight, and give orange pictures if used under indoor household bulbs. Other films are balanced to give the right colours with tungsten lamps, but give blue pictures when used in daylight. Still other films are not meant for purely visible light at all, but are also sensitive to infra-red which we cannot see. You can get some interesting effects from using tungsten balanced film, and infra-red sensitive film, under normal daylight or electronic flash lighting.

The success of this picture lies in its bold cropping and composition. Photograph by Jon Tarrant, printed by Larry Bartlett.

Tungsten balanced films

Tungsten films (Kodak EPT160, and Scotch 640T for example) are supplied and processed just like any other 35mm slide film. If they are exposed in daylight or with normal electronic flash, the photographs will have an overall blue cast. But for more impact, try using both blue light (daylight or electronic flash) and orange light (bulbs or filtered flash) in the same picture.

A particularly successful technique is to fit an orange filter (85A tungsten-to-daylight conversion type) over a flashgun, then use it as a foreground light. (This is not the same as fill-in flash, where the flash is actually less powerful than the available light). In this case the lens should be set to exactly the aperture as the flashgun requires when it is set to the same ISO as the film rating. To avoid having the slides rather too thin, it is advisable to under-develop the film (pull the development) by the equivalent of approximately 1 f-stop. The result is a picture where the flash-lit area has a normal colour balance, whereas the background is distinctly blue. This is particularly appropriate for portraits, where you may well want to render the subject's skin tones accurately, whilst altering the background.

The larger photograph was taken using Kodak Ektachrome Infra-red film without filters, and developed using the modified E6 process. The smaller picture shows how the model appeared on conventional film.

Another property of the tungsten films is that they give lower contrast results than normal film when used under daylight conditions. By fitting the same 85A orange filter over the camera lens it is possible to take daylight pictures with a normal colour balance, but taking advantage of the film's lower contrasts.

Infra-red films

There is only one type of colour infra-red film available in the UK, manufactured by Kodak. The main drawback to it is that it is intended for processing in E4 chemistry, which is now almost obsolete. If you do your own processing, it can also be developed using a modified version of the

common E6 process. Use both developers at one third of their normal strength, and do all the processing at 20° C. First development will take about 30 minutes, followed by colour development for about 20 minutes. Fixing is done at normal strength for 10 minutes. As usual, there should be washes between each stage to avoid cross contamination of the chemicals.

Pictures taken on Ektachrome Infra-red film, have distorted colours, including skin tones, but it is difficult to predict what the distortion will be, since it depends on the reflection of infra-red as well as visible light. It is normal to fit a yellow filter when photographing skin tones, but even this is not essential, depending on the effect required.

In addition to the colour slide film, there are also black and white infra-red films, which distort tones rather than colours. Kodak make a 35mm film, and Konica make a 120 roll film – although the latter can be difficult to obtain. Both can be developed in normal black and white chemicals, including Kodak D-76/Ilford ID-11 developers. They can be used in the same way as the colour version, with a yellow filter, or with no filter at all. Or, for really dramatic results, they can be exposed purely by

infra-red light. A special filter (Kodak Wratten No. 87, or equivalent) is used to block out all visible light, though this is difficult to work with because the filter is opaque, so you can't see through the camera lens to keep an eye on what you're photographing.

Using grain for effect
Modern films are rapidly becoming so good that it can be difficult to get a nice gritty effect when a subject calls for it. Kodak T-MAX P3200 is the answer for black and white. With its 3200 ISO rating, the negatives have a well-defined grain pattern whilst the film is still able to keep plenty of detail and sharpness. Although intended for sports and presss work, the film can also give exciting portraits.

For colour transparencies, Agfachrome 1000 and Scotch 1000 stand alone as grainy soft-coloured films well suited to high key pastel subjects with a predominance of light tones. All the other high-speed slide films, including Scotch P800/3200, are the modern type, which give very bright colours and high contrast. They tend to be rather sterile by comparison with the old-fashioned versions.

The best colour film for grain prints is Konica's SR-G3200 which is available in both 35mm and 120 roll film.

If you are using grain for effect, you can ignore the suggestions given in chapter 10 about how to minimise it. In fact, you can then do the opposite if you really want to accentuate the grain, but be careful that the subject is appropriate to this technique. The approach is similar to the pointilistic style of painting, so you could check out artists such as Paul Signach and George Suerat for suitable ideas.

Subduing colours

The problem of bright colours also extends to colour print films. Whilst these colours may be accurate, they look out of place in a picture which is

The picture with the darker dress was taken unfiltered on Kodak B/W Infra-red film. The other picture was taken a few moments later using a Wratten 87 Infra-red filter, which blocks all visible light. The dress was actually made of a matt black material.

meant to have a more old-fashioned feel. This can be overcome by under-exposing the film, but with an attendant loss of shadow detail and black density. The highlights also become slightly dulled. It is a technique best done on softer 400 ISO films, because brighter, slower speed, films tend to lose overall quality faster than the colours dull.

Mixing sharpness and blur

We have already mentioned combining flash and daylight for filling-in shadows, and for providing localised orange light when tungsten film is used. There is yet another use, which is to give a mixture of sharpness and blur when photographing action subjects.

The technique of mixing flash and blur is usually known as slow sync flash, because it involves setting the camera to a shutter speed slower than the usual flash speed. Often the shutter will be set to about 1/15 second, which would give considerable blur for most moving subjects. The aperture needs to be set as required for the flashgun power, and flash to subject distance. But this also needs to be about 1 f-stop smaller than the aperture required to balance the shutter speed for the available light. Working in diffused daylight, and using ISO 100 film, the available light exposure would probably be about f/16 at 1/15 second. The lens would therefore need to be set to f/22, and the flashgun would have to supply sufficient power for this to be the correct exposure for it alone. Even using a powerful flashgun, with a metre guide number of 45, it could be no more than 2 metres away from the subject. Less powerful flashguns would have to be correspondingly closer, according to the formula;

$$\text{Flash to subject distance} = \frac{\text{Flashgun guide number}}{\text{f-stop set on lens}}$$

Working at close range, and yet having to fill the frame with action, tends to favour wide-angle lenses. Sports such as cyclo-cross are particularly good for this technique.

Picture shapes

Negative shapes are determined by camera and film manufacturers, not by photographers. There is no reason to believe that they know what shapes your pictures should be better than you do. What is true, however, is that photographers tend to compose their pictures using the available format. A single scene would be photographed with different compositions by photographers using different film formats. It would be wrong, therefore, for somebody else to crop the images for an arbitrary reason – such as to fit a space on a page. This is now recognised in UK law, where the 1988 Copyright Act gives photographers the moral right not to have their pictures mutilated.

But for photographers printing their own pictures or getting them printed by a

Shot on colour negative film, the subdued colours have been achieved by deliberate underexposure. The overall result was enhanced by using soft, natural lighting from a large window, and by careful but informal posing.

commercial lab, there is no limit to how the image may be cropped to improve the result. This can even include circular or irregular cropping, to emphasise a fish-eye effect perhaps, or to isolate one element from a photograph. Similarly, finished photographs can be fashioned from a series of smaller pictures – as made

famous in David Hockney's "joiner" pictures which featured a mass of small Polaroids, each showing a small part of the total scene.

Damaging your work
Mention of cutting out parts of prints inevitably leads on to other sorts of creative damage that can be used for special

effects. Abrupt changes in temperature when processing films can cause reticulation, which gives a coarse pattern over the negatives – very much like an oversized grain pattern. Subjecting finished transparencies to heat causes bubbling of the emulsion, which again gives a pattern overlaid on the original image. And soaking black and white prints in tea can be used as a tinting technique.

On a slightly less dramatic scale, films meant for development in one process can often be put through another to achieve a particular effect. We have already said that Ektachrome infra-red film can go through a modified E6 process, instead of E4. Normal colour slide films (meant for E6) can be run through the C-41 process designed for colour negative films. This gives very high contrast, and distortion of blues and greens, but is otherwise quite predictable. The result is negatives, even though the film was intended for slides. This is actually rather convenient because it means that colour casts can be corrected at the printing stage.

A standard b/w negative was printed onto very high contrast (orthochromatic) paper, then the print was cut up and stuck down onto bright green card.

THE ONE REALLY UNBREAKABLE RULE

The one unbreakable rule we have is about editing your work. Only ever show people your best photographs, and don't include pictures for which you feel a need to apologise. If you know that the picture could have been better, then go out and do it better. This also gives you the freedom to experiment. If something doesn't work, only you will have seen it.

Nowhere is this more true than when attempting alternative pictures – because it is essential that they really do look alternative, and not just like mistakes. Be bold in what you do, and only show it to the rest of the world when you've got it right.

Guideline	Alternative
Compose with important elements lying on thirds of the picture	Place people at the edges of the picture for very unbalanced compositions
You must always show a person's head and eyes	Crop just the middle of a body if, for example, a uniform is most important
Choose film to match the type of lighting being used	Use tungsten balanced film outdoors for blue tones
Use the slowest film speed practicable to make the grain as unobtrusive as possible	Kodak T-MAX P3200 can be used for high contrast pictures with gritty grain
It is better to over-expose colour print films to get brilliant colours	Under-expose by one or two f-stops to subdue colours
Select fast shutter speeds for sharp pictures, and slow ones for creative blurs	Flash and bright light can give both sharpness and blur in the same picture
The perfectionist's approach to printing means not cropping the negative at all	There is nothing sacred about film formats. The print should match the subject, not a limitation built into the camera
A damaged slide or negative is useless for further work	Experiment with deliberate damage (gentle heat, or scratching) for effect

11: PROCESSING

INTRODUCTION

By far the majority of photographers do not process their own films or prints. Although it may provide another enjoyable facet to the hobby of photography, it can also be a burden to those whose first love is taking pictures. Because of this, and the complexity of detailing all the aspects of home processing, this chapter is devoted to getting the best from commercial processors.

GETTING FILMS PROCESSED

When you get your pictures back from a commercial laboratory, you should examine the results for processing quality, as well as for your own techniques. Transparencies are particularly critical, because processed film is the end result, and there is little possibility of correcting any faults.

Transparency processing

In theory, colours in transparencies should be an exact match of reality. This is rarely the case, because film manufacturers play around with the emulsion to enhance the blueness of the sky, or to give extra warmth to skin tones. Variations in processing can also cause accidental colour shifts. It is a good idea to photograph a test subject on each roll of film, and compare the processed results with the original. By doing this on the same kind of film, and using different processing laboratories, you can see what the variations are.

The test subject needs to include a range of colours, both vivid and pastel, as well as black, white and grey. You can get purpose designed cards which often feature an area where you can write your name and address for identification. Colour cards used for matching paints are a rough alternative. When comparing the original with the transparency, it is important to use the correct light source – ideally this should be a daylight balanced light box. Look carefully at the colours and densities, and also at whether there is a colour cast in grey areas.

Unfortunately, there is very little you can do about poor transparency processing, except to bring it to the attention of the laboratory concerned, and avoid that lab in the future.

If you have used your film under non-standard conditions, such as under- or over-exposing, then over- or under-developing to compensate, you cannot expect the colours to remain completely faithful. But this test is still useful because it shows exactly what changes will occur, both in terms of density and colours. It also demonstrates the increase in graininess associated with under exposure and over development. This technique is called 'pushing', and is used when there is not enough light to expose the film normally.

Colour print processing
Things are very much less critical with colour prints, because the film is only an intermediate stage, and there is the chance to remake prints as many times as is required to get them exactly right. This assumes, of course, that the negatives are clean and free from scratches – which should

be your first concern. As it happens, even cheap mini-labs are capable of producing good negatives, although their prints often leave something to be desired. Given that you can get reprints, or enlargements, of your favorite pictures, it makes good sense to use cheap processing simply as a way of getting rough prints which show what you have in the negatives.

Getting accurate colours is much harder when printing from negatives, than it is when developing or printing transparency film. The reason for this is that it is not possible to compare the print directly with the negative. Whilst there may be sky, grass or skin tones

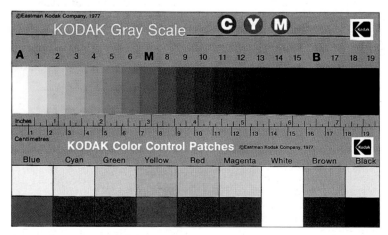

Reproduction of Kodak Colour Card, suitable for checking film and processing quality. Original cards are available from major photographic suppliers – ref Kodak Publication Q-13.

which indicate what the correct colours should be, there are many shades of blue, green and flesh tones that could be right. A test subject is helpful here, because by including a complete colour card the processor will be able to set an exact colour balance for your film. Even so, you cannot expect the prints to be perfect, because the colour balance is set for the entire roll, rather than for individual frames.

Common processing faults include colour casts, often magenta or blue, and prints lacking in clean whites or deep blacks. But remember that the film must have been correctly exposed to get the best results, and that while colour print films can withstand substantial exposure errors before showing serious loss of quality, any inaccuracy in exposure will have some effect. That said, if you feel that your film has been badly printed, ask for it to be redone – even if you know the prints are only for rough use.

Black and white processing

Getting black and white films processed can be difficult, and even when you find a lab willing to do the film, you may find the prints are of poor quality. There are two possible ways around this. The first option is to send your films to a high quality mail order laboratory – who charge about the same for black and white or colour, but who are rather more expensive than a local mini-lab. The second option is to use Ilford XP2, a black and white film that can be developed and printed by conventional colour mini-labs. XP2 can, of course, be printed onto conventional black and white paper too – and so can normal black and white films be printed onto colour paper, for special effects.

Printing black and white on colour paper, whether it is XP2 or normal film, gives prints which are not truly black and white, but which often have a slight colour cast. This is perfectly normal, and often adds to the feel of the pictures, which is why you might want to try getting a local mini-lab to do some of your black and whites. If the lab is particularly co-operative, you could actually ask them for a residual sepia colour cast, to give the pictures an old fashioned feel. You could suggest other casts too, and save yourself messing around with toners.

REPRINTS AND ENLARGEMENTS

There is a crucial difference in what you can expect from normal film processing and from reprints or enlargements.

As has already been stated, films are normally processed using average colour corrections, with automatic adjustments as the printing machine sees fit. Reprints and enlargements, on the other hand, should be given individual attention, and it is reasonable to expect the results to be as perfect as possible. Exactly how perfect this is depends on the negative, and the type of printing requested.

Top printer, Larry Bartlett, was given free rein to produce the best result possible of this 105 year old woman. The finished print should be compared with the contact to appreciate how the image has been manipulated to bring out the best, and how skillful printing has set the mood much more strongly than was apparent in the original negative. Border printing is an important part of print presentation – the white line on black seen here is distinctive of Larry Bartlett's work. The print was made on Ilford Multigrade III RC paper.

Machine prints
These are basically just like enprints, in that they are done using a similar automatic machine. But in this case, the results are inspected, and should be reprinted if there is any colour cast, or if the print is too light or too dark overall. The overall condition is important, because machine prints cannot be adjusted to take account of localised areas of the negative. Prints are often fixed sizes, with only the most minimal opportunity for cropping unwanted parts of the picture – if any such options are available at all. Machine prints should be regarded as straightforward copies of the negative, but they should be technically perfect nevertheless.

Hand prints
There are two categories of hand prints. The first is basically just a manual version of machine prints, where an operator positions paper under the enlarger, but is still making a straightforward print – although there is usually more flexibility for having the

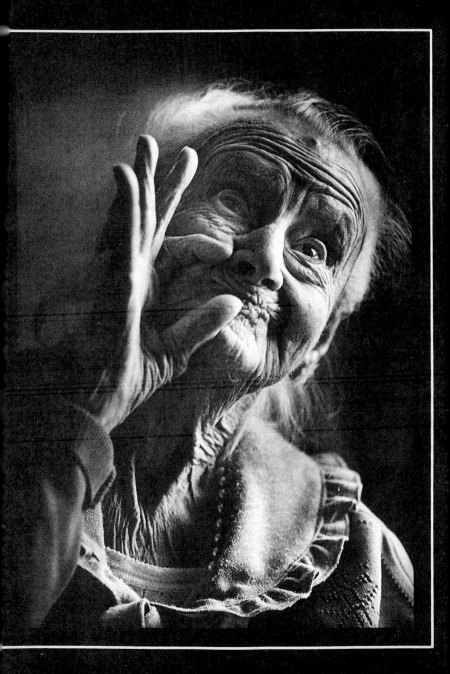

XP1 (recently replaced by XP2) is a b/w film which can be processed and printed using colour chemicals and paper to produce either b/w or toned results. It is not possible to get true black and white – as the bottom right print (which was the most neutral) shows. Toned results are a matter for experimentation, and it may prove impossible to match the tones obtained on a previous occasion. This gives the prints a certain degree of uniqueness. XP1 can also be printed onto normal black and white paper to give traditional monochrome results. Original photograph by Cathy Corr, all printing by Fotostop Express (Tolworth), Surrey.

negative cropped. The other type of hand printing is the most useful, and requires a very skilled operator. Here, parts of the negative can be printed differently from the rest. This is most useful for darkening light areas in a technique called 'burning-in', or lightening dark areas called 'shading'. It should come as no surprise to learn that hand printing is more expensive than machine prints – at least twice the price, and sometimes very much more.

Unfortunately, many people go for hand printing not because their negatives need special treatment, but because the machine prints are of such low quality. This is a total waste of money, and represents the laboratory taking advantage of its customers. You would be better advised to hunt around for a good machine printing lab, than fund a poor quality one by having hand prints done.

Prints from slides

Slides are very inconvenient when it comes to displaying the pictures. The original choice to use slide film, in preference to print film, doesn't mean that prints cannot be made from slides – but it is a process which has its problems. Slides tend to have much more contrast than negatives, and since papers which give bright prints are of high contrast themselves, there is a very real danger that the total contrast will cause areas of burnt-out highlights and blocked-up shadows. Fortunately, there are several different types of paper for doing prints from slides, and some cope better with contrast than others.

The most brilliant material is Ilford Cibachrome, available in both its original form and a low contrast version to accommodate high contrast slides. Whilst Cibachrome is probably the best paper in terms of really punchy colours and a good range of densities, it is also rather expensive. Kodak and Fuji both make alternative materials, and Fuji's Super Gloss paper gives particularly well finished results – with a price tag midway between normal materials and Cibachromes.

Another possibility for displaying slides is to get them enlarged onto transparency film. This really is an exotic move, and requires the purchase of a slimline illuminated panel on which to mount the results. But for the right picture, the effect can be stunning. It is very similar to looking at stained glass, and is most suited to very colourful subjects which have no large areas of white, or other light tones.

The instructions here were to remove the distracting pair of legs from the background of this photograph.

Telling a lab what you want

When getting hand printing done, it is not enough just to describe what you want. It is far better to make a sketch, or mark off on the rough print what is required. Be as exact as possible, avoiding general comments such as 'make darker'. It is better to give an indication of how dark – either with reference to the existing density ('make twice as dark as this'), or by comparison with another area ('darken to match indicated area'), or with a view to the desired effect ('darken to show detail clearly'). The laboratory will be grateful for precise instructions, and you are more likely to get exactly what you were after.

Hand prints can be cropped according to your specifications. This gives you the chance to concentrate on the most important part of the picture, or to change the shape of the image to improve the composition. Again, the best way of instructing the lab is to mark the rough print. Bear in mind that the cropped area should have the same proportions as the paper onto which it will be printed. If this is not the case then the lab may well print more than your indicated area, and leave you to trim the result. Alternatively, they may mask off the area specified, and the final print will have large white borders where the image didn't fill the paper.

If you are only getting a hand print made to satisfy a cropping scheme, you might be better off getting an oversize machine print done, then trimming the picture yourself. This is almost always a cheaper alternative, provided you can cut the print without damaging it. Scissors are not suitable, and it is better to use a sharp modelling knife guided by a steel rule, both of which are available from art shops.

A printer's photograph

All the previous comments have assumed that you, the

The lab was asked to process slide film through negative chemicals and then to provide a conventional print to give very high contrast and bright colours.

photographer, know what is best for your pictures. But this is not always the case. Top photographic printers are experts in their field, and their experience with thousands of other negatives means they often know exactly how to get the best from your work. Their ideas may well be different from your own, because they have a different approach to negatives, but it is very likely that the results could be better than you ever thought possible.

The very best printers can be identified by the style of their prints even though the original pictures may have been taken by a variety of photographers, each with their own style. Ideally, the printer's style should complement the photographer's. Such pictures are likely to be of the very highest standard, and it is no coincidence that many award winning photographs are produced by a professional photographers working with professional printers.

12: STORAGE AND PRESENTATION

STORING NEGATIVES

You need to consider two factors when storing your negatives; protecting them and finding them again. For negatives to be safe, they should be kept in the dark and contained so they cannot get scratched or dusty. The type of filing system you use to do this will depend on how many pictures you take and on what kind of film.

For print films that have been processed by a lab, you can keep the negatives with enprints in their wallets. The wallets are easy to label and fairly easy to stack. However, when you start to build up a large collection which you refer to a lot, it can be tedious to search through each wallet in turn. And if you do your own processing, you won't have wallets, so will need to find another means of storage.

Negative filing ring binders are particularly versatile. As well as the pages for storing negatives, you can get plastic wallets for prints, and pages for holding mounted slides. Large numbers of prints become very bulky, so it is better to file a contact sheet if possible. These also have the advantage of identifying the negative number of each picture, something which is much more difficult with loose prints. The binders come with index pages and it is easy to label the

The contrast between orange and black in the mounting is in keeping with the moody portrait of a teenager.

inserted pages, making everything very quick to find when needed.

STORING SLIDES

Slide films are usually mounted and stored in plastic boxes. The boxes are easy to stack and label, but again become bulky and tedious to look through when your collection starts to build up. While it is possible to file mounted slides, this can become almost as bulky as filing prints. It is better to ask the lab not to mount the slides, so that you can cut the films into five- or six-frame lengths and store them just like negatives.

In order to minimise the risk of damage, you should look through your films as little as possible. This makes a good filing system important. You can, for example, use one binder for each subject, children, family, events and so on, then file negatives in date order in each binder. If the binders themselves are labelled carefully, and the indices kept up to date, you should be able to lay your hands on any particular negative without disturbing too many others. The main thing is to create a filing system that you find easy to maintain.

PRESENTATION

Taking, processing and printing your photographs are intermediate steps towards the final presentation. As you want your pictures to be seen and admired, it is important that the final presentation does justice to all the preceding hard work. There are many ways to display your portraits, depending on their type, and whether you want to show them individually or as a collection.

ALBUMS

Albums are a convenient way to display large numbers of pictures, making it very tempting to include every photograph you have ever taken. Don't. Be ruthlessly selective. Your work will appear to its best advantage if you include only your very best shots. There is also a psychological factor, in that if you know you don't have to show your failures to anyone, you are more likely to push yourself to try difficult ideas.

Types of albums
There are all sorts of albums on the market, from little ones that hold enprints, to large glossy albums where you insert more pages as you need them. When buying an album, check the page size and the method of fixing prints to see how suitable it is for your particular purpose. You may want to create a family chronicle and find a large album with loose leaf pages would give you the flexibility you need. Or you may want to circulate a collection of wedding pictures, in which case a small album with plastic pockets will be easy to pass around and will offer plenty of protection against careless handling.

Contact sheets are easy to store and make selecting reprints simple.

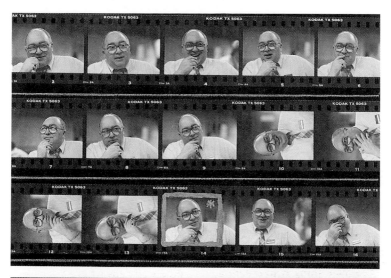

*Old fashioned frames are most suited to old fashioned pictures.
In this case, the entire effect has been created by make-up and a
real location, then toning the print. Model; Yvonne Covus.
Make-up; Melissa Lackersteen. Photograph by Jon Tarrant.
Printed and toned by Larry Bartlett.*

Organising an album

It is far more interesting to
look through an album where
the pictures are presented in
an organised way. You could
use a small album to tell the
story of a particular event, such
as a day at the races or a party.
In either of these cases, you
might display them in
chronological order. If, on the
other hand, you were
collecting pictures of churches
then you might choose to
order them alphabetically by
location.

Perhaps the most common
use for albums is to keep a
record of the family.
Chronological order is the
most usual for a family album,
but it is by no means the only
possibility. You might want to
show pictures of different
generations on one page to
bring out family resemblances.
Or you could show how
everyone looked at age three.

One page might show the family cars over the years or how a garment that was handed down looked on different members of the family. For this kind of collection, it is a good idea to look for an album that allows you to move prints easily.

Be imaginative with print sizes and shapes. If you want to crop a print, remember you do not necessarily have to cut in straight lines. You can get interesting results by cutting round a head, for example. There is no reason why you should not mix different print sizes and black and white and colour on the same page, provided that it doesn't look untidy.

FRAMES

You may well want to frame your very best portraits and keep them on permanent display. Frames can be used to show off one or several prints. When choosing a frame, you need to consider where the picture will go and what kind of portrait it will contain.

Frames for displaying on shelves
If you want a frame to go on a shelf, a good size would be 8" × 10", either with the print occupying the whole area, or perhaps with a small border within the frame. You can buy ready made borders, in the form of overlays or 'mattes' that will fit inside standard frames. They can be very useful for isolating your subject or for hiding distracting backgrounds that may show at the edges of the picture. Be careful about how much is covered up, though. You could ruin a picture by leaving the odd twig showing where the matte does not quite fit.

Frames for displaying on walls
The minimum size for wall display is about 11" × 14", and you can go right up to 30" × 40" or larger – depending on the wall area you are trying to fill and the content of the picture. If you have a really spectacular photograph, you might want to get a large print canvas-bonded and make it the centrepiece of your room. But be certain that the negative quality is impeccable before getting larger prints done, as every fault will be magnified.

The frame you choose must not only suit the print, but also the room it will be in. A framed portrait is, after all, part of the decor. There is an enormous variety of frames available, from the glass clip frame to ornate silver frames. A modern, stylish black and white portrait might suit a glass frame, whilst a sepia toned print would look better in a more old-fashioned type of frame. You can buy frames

139

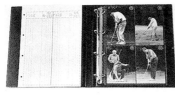

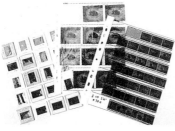

A selection of pages available for photographic filing binders.

from specialist shops or photographic suppliers. It is also worth exploring antique shops, if you want a genuine old frame.

Displaying multiple prints

You have a number of options if you want to display more than one print in a frame. Photocubes, which hold six small prints, make good desk ornaments. Hinged frames are good for standing on mantelpieces and you can also get wall mounted frames that hold several pictures. Alternatively, you can get a masking card for displaying different size prints in a single frame.

As with albums, it is more interesting to have a common factor when displaying several pictures together. For example, you could have four small headshots and a larger full length portrait of the same person in a hinged frame on a mantelpiece.

MOUNTING PRINTS

Mounting your pictures gives them extra support, and is especially useful for larger prints to go on the wall. You can simply mount the print flush onto a piece of card or you can use a border to enhance it. This is particularly important if you are using a glass clip frame, because they have no borders of their own, so the print mounting style should include one if it is required.

It is worth experimenting with different width borders, but a good starting point is to use a border of about one-tenth of the longest dimension of the print. So for a 12″ × 16″ print, you could leave a border of 1.5″ to 2″ all round. A 2″ border would give a mounted picture exactly the right size for a standard 16″ × 20″ frame.

Make sure that the colour of the card is appropriate to the print, either being neutral, matching, complementary, or picking up an element from within the picture itself. White is always a safe bet. Black is slightly less so, but both are rather sterile and should be considered as somewhat conservative.

The most convenient way of sticking prints onto card is to use an adhesive spray. However, these are unpleasant to use as they are unhealthy for you and for the environment, so try to use them as sparingly as possible. There are two types to choose from, one being more permanent, but less repositionable, than the other.

For your first attempts it is as well to use a spray which allows you to move the print slightly after it has been lightly pressed down. When the print is properly in position, cover it with a piece of white paper and press it down with a wallpaper roller. Once the print is firmly stuck, you can trim the card using a rotary cutter or a sharp knife guided by a steel rule. It is much easier to stick the print onto an oversized piece of card then to trim it, than to do it the other way around and try to get the print exactly in the middle of a previously cut piece of card. Throughout the whole operation, it is essential that all your equipment is scrupulously clean to avoid marking the print.

SLIDE SHOWS

Slide shows are most often associated with holidays, but there is no reason why you shouldn't put together a collection of portraits. A reasonable length would be twenty to thirty slides each shown for about half a minute, depending on how interesting the subject is to your audience. Make sure you have something to say about each slide, and that they are of good technical quality.

As with an album, a slide show will be much more interesting if it is organised coherently. Slide shows are very good for telling stories, such as a day out or lunch with baby. It is a good idea to have START and END slides. You can make the titles more fun by making them part of the show. For example, if you have a sequence of a child, you can photograph the child holding the titles, or perhaps wearing them like a sandwich board.

You can also add sound by using a stereo tape deck and a slide synchroniser. Try experimenting with environmental sounds, rather than a spoken commentary. Children are particularly good for this; you could get snatches of their conversations or record sounds from a playground or a baby's gurgles.

When giving a slide show, you do not have to stick to the slide projector and screen. It is now possible to get small table top projectors with a built-in screen. They are much easier to set up, less bulky, and are better suited to small groups of people.

PORTFOLIOS

A portfolio is designed to display your skill as a photographer, and as such it should include only your finest work. There are a number of ways you can put a portfolio together, but it is important that you allow yourself the flexibility to change pictures so that you always have your best current pictures.

You don't need to have a large number of pictures in your portfolio. Ten excellent prints are far better than ten excellent ones diluted with ten mediocres. At the same time, it is important that the pictures in your portfolio look as if they belong together. One way to do this is to standardise your mounting. Also, beware of having just one colour picture with nine black and whites or only one group portrait where the rest are singles.

Prints easily get tatty, so make sure your portfolio is well protected. You can get display binders designed for twenty A4 sized documents in plastic pockets. They are ideal for holding ten photographs, one per pocket, as they allow the prints to be seen whilst

offering protection. It is better not to put two pictures back to back in each pocket, both because of the bulk it creates and the fact that the two facing pictures on each page would have to be completely harmonious with each other.

If you want to keep your pictures loose, it is a good idea to have them laminated, and to store them in an artist's folder. This allows greater flexibility in print size and number of prints. However, there is no need for prints to be very large, unless size enhances them.

Why a portfolio is important
However you decide to present your portfolio, you should make sure that you have some sort of collection of your best pictures. This is as much for your benefit as anybody else's. There will be times when nothing goes right, and every exciting idea you have seems to end in failure. It is very cheering to turn to your portfolio, and remind yourself how good things can look when they turn out as planned. And over the years, your portfolio becomes an interesting record of how your technical ability has improved, and how your style has changed.

TO FIND OUT MORE

Finally, we would like to offer a few suggestions as to how you can find out more to help you with your photography. We cannot be specific about suppliers of equipment and information, as these vary so much over time and location. The major equipment and materials manufacturers all have information services. You can often find their details from local photographic dealers. Many professional photographic magazines publish annual directories which list suppliers of equipment and materials. Certain items can still be difficult to track down (for example, we have only been able to find screw fit Softar filters at Teamwork in Covent Garden, London), but the majority of distributors and suppliers can easily be found.

For practical advice on photography, your local camera club is a good starting point. And to find your local camera club, try the library or an amateur photographers' magazine. On a larger scale, there is the Royal Photographic Society, based in Bath, which caters for all kinds of photographers all over the world. One of the best ways to assess your work is to have it judged in one of the many competitions and exhibitions held each year. Again, photographic magazines are an ideal source of information about entry requirements and closing dates.

ACKNOWLEDGEMENTS

The authors would like to thank all those who have contributed to this book. Special thanks are due to Kate Wilson and the photographers who participated in the 'style' project, and to Larry Bartlett for his examples of printing excellence. We would also like to pay tribute to the late Ron Franks FRPS, who provided much help and encouragement to Jon Tarrant through his involvement at The Camera Club, London.

All the photographs in this book were taken by Jon Tarrant, except for those listed below:

Rachel Braverman   Trevor Spiro
Cathy Corr   Ian Banister
Brian Fanning   Jon Gadd
Paul Barsby   Fuji Photo Film (UK) Ltd.
Naina Khambhaita   P.L. Hartley

Make-up by Melissa Lackersteen and Mandy Tenalver. Principal models – Yvonne Covus and Krystyna Zukowska.

INDEX